US Elections & Voting Behaviour

Edward Ashbee

Series editor
Eric Magee

Philip Allan Updates
Market Place
Deddington
Oxfordshire
OX15 0SE

Orders
Bookpoint Ltd, 130 Milton Park, Abingdon, Oxfordshire, OX14 4SB
tel: 01235 827720
fax: 01235 400454
e-mail: uk.orders@bookpoint.co.uk
Lines are open 9.00 a.m.–5.00 p.m., Monday to Saturday, with a 24-hour
message answering service. You can also order through the Philip Allan Updates
website:
www.philipallan.co.uk

Printed in Spain

Environmental information
Philip Allan Updates' policy is to use papers that are natural, renewable
and recyclable products and made from wood grown in sustainable forests.
The logging and manufacturing processes are expected to conform to the
environmental regulations of the country of origin.

Contents

Introduction

We inevitably think about the US political process, and elections in particular, through European eyes. However, there is a twist: in practice, we often use a model of European politics that could have been useful some decades ago but has rather less relevance or legitimacy today.

Differences between the US and European political process

As a consequence, trans-Atlantic differences are often underestimated. You may see the two major US parties, the Republicans and Democrats, and assume that they are broadly comparable with the Conservative and Labour parties or, to adopt a more broadly European perspective, the Christian democrats and social democrats. Against this background, President Bill Clinton is regarded as a left-winger, particularly when seen in contrast with George W. Bush. Similarly, familiar with the defining features of European politics, you may assume that the principal US parties are highly structured and disciplined membership organisations with recognised and acknowledged leaders. You might believe that these members and leaders are the people who pick the candidates who stand for election at federal, state and local level. You hear the word 'whips' and assume that 'whipping' in Congress is a similar process to that used in the House of Commons. Furthermore, despite the controversies about 'partisan dealignment' and the recent policy lurches of the Labour and Conservative parties, you may think of the US parties in class — or socioeconomic — terms. The Democrats are seen as the party of the poor, while the Republicans, it is said, represent the interests of the wealthy.

Partisan dealignment refers to the decline in the proportion of party 'identifiers'. The concept suggests that as long-term attachments to the parties have weakened, there is greater electoral volatility, and short-term variables such as the character of the campaigns have begun to play more of a role. In the USA, the evidence for partisan dealignment is patchy. There was some alienation from established politics and parties during the 1970s in the aftermath of the Vietnam war and the Watergate scandal. There have also been long-term shifts away from the Democrats by important groups of voters and the party no longer secures the level of support that it enjoyed in the 1960s. Nonetheless, Republican identification is still at about the same level that it was several decades ago. And, in

the 2004 election, there often seemed to be a bitter divide between supporters of the major parties.

Of course, there is some validity in these points. There is a relationship in the USA as well as Europe between an individual's income level and the way in which he or she votes. Those at the lower end of the scale are disproportionately more likely to vote for the Democrats (although, as you will discover, significant numbers of low-income whites, particularly those with few or no educational qualifications, have defected to the Republicans in recent years). There are, furthermore, signs of centralisation in the US party system. Indeed, until his poll ratings plummeted during 2005 and early 2006, President Bush was more of a party leader than many other presidents. The Bush White House has worked closely with the Republican leadership in Congress and the party's legislative efforts have often been well coordinated. Leading figures in both parties have sought to ensure that their preferred candidate was picked to fight particular House or Senate races on behalf of the party. The parties' Congressional campaign committees have played a pivotal role in directing efforts towards particular races.

At the same time, there have been parallel developments on this side of the Atlantic. The electoral process in Britain (and some other European countries) has become more 'American'. Candidates have been selected on the basis of a substantially widened franchise. Within Parliament, there have been some powerful displays of independence by backbenchers. Furthermore, although theorists used to contrast the 'ideological' character of European parties with the US parties, which they depicted as broad 'non-ideological' coalitions, it is difficult to employ these terms in an era when both Tony Blair and David Cameron seem, to the chagrin of some grassroots activists, to have abandoned many of their parties' traditional and most deeply embedded beliefs.

Nonetheless, it would be a mistake to forget the differences between US and European electoral politics. As you will see, the US electoral system remains much more 'open'. This openness allowed relative outsiders such as Jimmy Carter, Ronald Reagan, Bill Clinton and George W. Bush to secure their party's presidential nomination and then win the White House. All four state governors 'leapfrogged' over experienced and seasoned politicians who had served for many years in the US Congress. For better or worse, the openness of the process also permits relatively small and perhaps unrepresentative groupings, such as the Christian right, to sway the primary process through which parties select their candidates.

The **Christian right** (which sometimes calls itself 'the pro-family movement') refers to organisations such as the Family Research Council, the Traditional Values Coalition and Concerned Women for America. They draw much of their support from white evangelical Protestants and are a core constituency within the Republican Party. They call for the adoption of policies based upon 'family values' or moral traditionalism. These include opposition to abortion, the prohibition of same-sex marriage and curbs on television programming. The Christian right has been politically influential since the late 1970s.

Furthermore, despite European perceptions, the Democrats are not a labour or social-democratic party. Although the electoral coalition that backed the Democrats has included large numbers of blue-collar (or manual) workers since the 1930s, there were also (at least until the 1960s) white southerners who were committed to the maintenance of racial segregation within its ranks. In contrast with the European left, the Democrats have never embraced an alternative economic order, a radical redistribution of income and wealth, or had close formal links with the trade unions. For his part, Bill Clinton won the White House on the basis of a platform that included support for the death penalty and a commitment to a toughened system of welfare provision. During the campaign, he deliberately and pointedly distanced himself from black radicalism.

Detractors and admirers

The US electoral system has both detractors and admirers. Its presidential elections have at times seemed to be contests between unattractive and under-qualified candidates. At the time of the 1980 presidential election, for example, commentators questioned the abilities of both Jimmy Carter, the incumbent president, and Ronald Reagan, the Republican challenger. Carter's period of office had often been troubled and gave rise to talk of an 'impaired' or even 'imperiled' presidency. Although Reagan was later to be hailed by many conservatives as a presidential giant who led the USA to victory in the Cold War, he seemed at that time to be ideologically extreme and to possess a profoundly reckless streak. He was dismissed by some European observers as a simple 'cowboy'. Later candidates, including both Bill Clinton and George W. Bush, also attracted criticism. Both were at different times said to be inexperienced and unsuited for high office. In particular (and this is a charge that is always levelled at state governors seeking the presidency), it was often noted that they lacked experience of foreign and defence policy.

Why, according to these commentators, did such 'unstatesmanlike' figures become presidential candidates? Some pointed to the character of American political culture. Ronald Reagan, it has been said, was popular because his evocation of cowboy culture and his identification with California and the 'sunbelt' seemed to capture the American spirit. Furthermore, as a former film actor, he was a political outsider. American culture celebrates the outsider who overcomes the obstacles placed in his way. However, other observers stress the role played by the defining features of the electoral system and point to its relative openness. In contrast with most European systems, it places 'insiders' and 'outsiders' on a more or less level playing field.

There are other criticisms of the US electoral process. Both money and the media are said to play too much of a role. Although the Federal Election Campaign Act established spending limits for presidential candidates in both primaries and the November election, these can be 'by-passed' if a candidate chooses not to take the funding offered (as an incentive) by the Federal Election Commission (FEC). As you will see, increasing numbers of candidates have chosen not to take funding in the primary contests and their spending has therefore been largely unregulated. Other commentators have pointed to the part played by the cable news channels. In contrast with UK television news coverage, there is no requirement for 'balance' between candidates, parties and points of view. In the USA, *Fox News* has, in particular, pioneered abrasively right-wing forms of programming that leave little room for doubt about the partisan allegiance of news 'anchors' and commentators.

Despite all these claims, however, other commentators have painted a much more sympathetic portrait. There are many opportunities for political partici-pation. Party supporters can vote for the candidates in federal, state and local elections. The key decisions are not made by small groups of unrepresentative organisers and activists. In the USA, candidate recruitment is open and sometimes unpredictable. In the UK, the recruitment 'pool' for the premiership is confined, in practice, to just two people: the leaders of the Labour and Conservative parties. Arguably, US candidates are 'tested' much more thoroughly than those seeking office in Britain. And, in many ways, campaign finance regulation is more rigorous in the USA than in Britain, as the allegations against party fundraisers in 2006 highlighted.

US Elections and Voting Behaviour provides a comprehensive picture of the electoral system and considers many of these criticisms. At the same time, it surveys the positive characteristics of the structures and processes that have been adopted in the USA. The book asks and seeks to answer some important questions. It considers the importance of the 'invisible primary'. How far are the parties' presidential nominees decided, in practice, well before the formal selection process begins? Commentators often make a case for reforming the primary and caucus system. They point, for example, to the disproportionate role played by unrepresentative states such as Iowa and New Hampshire. Are such criticisms justified?

The election campaigns attract widespread attention in both the USA and in other countries. However, do they really sway voters or, in an era of polarisation, are opinions already set in stone? Perhaps party election campaigns are now more a matter of 'energising the base' and maximising turnout among supporters? The 2000 presidential election led to some bitter comments about the Electoral College. It was said to be an undemocratic relic of an earlier age. Although the intensity of feeling has now been largely lost, the validity of comments such as these should still be considered.

Although we inevitably focus on presidential contests, what about Congressional elections? Elections to the House of Representatives are characterised, above all else, by the rate at which incumbents are repeatedly re-elected. Although Congress as a whole is often regarded with a degree of disdain, many voters have a degree of regard for their member of Congress and Senator. What are the reasons for this? Lastly, what factors shape voting behaviour? What is the relationship between long-term and short-term variables? How far do shifts in these variables explain George W. Bush's election victories?

The book is designed to build upon the coverage provided by A-level textbooks and journals such as *Politics Review*. It seeks to broaden students' knowledge and understanding of the subject while at the same time introducing them to key authors and core debates.

References are listed in the 'Further reading and references' section at the end of each chapter. Useful websites include:

- Democratic National Committee
  www.dnc.org
- Democratic Senatorial Campaign Committee
  www.dscc.org
- Democratic Congressional Campaign Committee
  www.dccc.org
- Republican National Committee
  www.rnc.org
- National Republican Senatorial Committee
  www.nrsc.org
- National Republican Congressional Committee
  www.nrcc.org
- The Center for Responsive Politics
  www.opensecrets.org
- Federal Election Commission
  www.fec.gov
- The Green Papers
  www.thegreenpapers.com
- Project Smart Vote
  www.vote-smart.org/index

Does the 'invisible primary' matter?

Chapter 1 considers the period preceding the beginning of the formal contest. It examines the process of informal and generally undeclared jostling as potential candidates seek to establish themselves before the beginning of the presidential race.

In the 1980s, studies of the US election system stressed the role of the early primaries and caucuses (particularly in Iowa and New Hampshire) in determining the winner of the race to secure the parties' presidential nominations. (Primaries and caucuses are contests that, although the procedures differ between states, enable registered party supporters to determine who should be selected as candidate.) These allowed relatively unknown figures to establish themselves in the initial contests and then, if they could convince the states' voters of their strengths, create a sense of momentum, secure funding, and attract influential backers so as to win the later primaries and emerge victorious at the end of the pre-nomination season that precedes the parties' national conventions. The process was likened to a snowball rolling down a hill.

Jimmy Carter's success in the 1976 Democratic primaries is cited as an illustration of this. He seemed to come from nowhere to win the initial primaries, build an effective national campaign, secure the Democratic nomination, and then capture the White House. (Carter's successes should not, however, be exaggerated. There was a crowded field of candidates in 1976 and Carter gained less than a third of the votes in Iowa and New Hampshire and only 39% of all the primary votes.)

The US primary system therefore seems to be characterised by an *openness* and *accessibility* that are absent in many other political

Jimmy Carter

systems in which the choice of candidates is much more limited. In Britain, for example, only leading parliamentarians can generally make a credible bid to lead their party (although David Cameron, who became Conservative Party leader in December 2005, had been an MP only since 2001). While there have been moves to broaden the franchise for electing party leaders, this is a relatively recent departure. Indeed, the Conservatives extended the right to vote for the party leader beyond their MPs only after the 1997 election defeat.

In more recent years, commentaries have begun to emphasise the importance of events and developments *before* the US primary season begins. There is a stress upon informal rather than formal processes that occur during the initial stages of what has become known as the 'invisible primary', a term coined by journalist William Mayer Arthur Hadley (see Box 1.1). At this stage, presidential candidates are often still undeclared or simply exploring the extent to which they might secure support. During the invisible primaries, instead of making a formal declaration, they often speak in a form of 'code' that enables them to establish a distinct political identity and place themselves in the electoral ring. They drop hints, leave questions about the subject open, or issue 'non-denials'. To an extent, they 'groom' party organisations across the country but most particularly in key primary states such as New Hampshire.

> **Box 1.1**
> **Tests of the invisible primary**
>
> Arthur Hadley argues that the 'invisible primary' was structured around six tests for candidates:
>
> (1) a 'psychological test' establishes whether a candidate has sufficient commitment and determination; (2) a 'staff test' assesses his or her ability to recruit and manage staff; (3) a 'strategy test' measures the extent to which the candidate has a credible plan through which to secure a place as a front-runner; (4) a 'money test' rests upon a candidate's fundraising abilities; (5) a 'media test' as a candidate strives to build a profile on the television and in the papers; and (6) the 'constituency test' assesses his or her ability to win a large, national team of supporters who will build and sustain a national campaign for the presidency.
>
> Cook (2003)

After the mid-term elections that take place 2 years before the presidential contest, there is a more open and pronounced jostling for position. Candidates establish exploratory committees or announce their intention to seek the presidency formally. They make every effort to secure name recognition, establish themselves in the public opinion polls, amass financial 'war chests', gain a foothold in key primary states, win endorsements from influential organisations and senior party figures, and ensure that they gain a credible vote in the 'straw polls' that are held at party gatherings or by some of the state parties.

Not every candidate in the 'invisible primary' and the formal primaries and caucuses is a serious contender for office. There are those who are fuelled by ideological zeal or hope to bolster their position within the party, at national, state or city level. The Revd Al Sharpton, a radical preacher and civil rights leader from New York, stood in the 2004 race for the Democratic nomination. He had no serious prospect of success and yet used the campaign to reinforce his role as a significant 'player' within the Democratic camp. Those seeking the African-American vote in New York must, sooner or later, establish a relationship with Sharpton.

What do public opinion polls contribute to the 'invisible primary'?

Newspaper and television networks' 'conduct polls' begin their polling long before the presidential elections. Such polls are a defining feature of the invisible primary in its earliest as well as its later stages. They simply ask respondents who should be elected as the next president on the basis of a list of names that often includes those who have no intention of seeking the presidency in addition to those who may be exploring the possibility of making a bid.

However, the value and reliability of the polls conducted before the mid-term elections are questionable. For instance, as you will see in Figures 1.1 and 1.2, in mid-November 2005 (a year ahead of the mid-term elections that preceded the 2008 presidential contest), pollsters asked about both Republicans and Democrats who might seek the presidency in 2008.

Task 1.1

Study Figures 1.1 and 1.2 and the information below each figure and then answer the questions that follow.

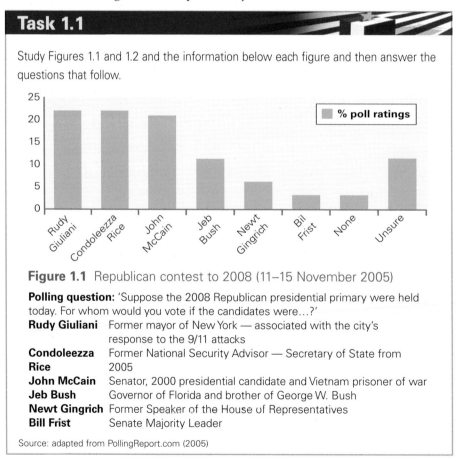

Figure 1.1 Republican contest to 2008 (11–15 November 2005)

Polling question: 'Suppose the 2008 Republican presidential primary were held today. For whom would you vote if the candidates were…?'

Rudy Giuliani Former mayor of New York — associated with the city's response to the 9/11 attacks
Condoleezza Rice Former National Security Advisor — Secretary of State from 2005
John McCain Senator, 2000 presidential candidate and Vietnam prisoner of war
Jeb Bush Governor of Florida and brother of George W. Bush
Newt Gingrich Former Speaker of the House of Representatives
Bill Frist Senate Majority Leader

Source: adapted from PollingReport.com (2005)

Task 1.1 (continued)

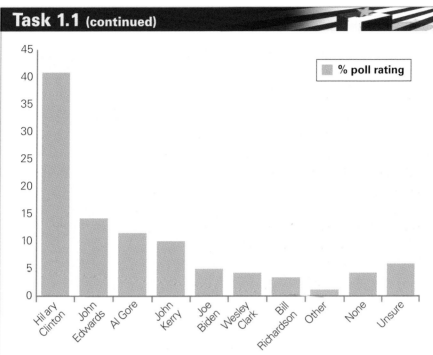

Figure 1.2 Democratic contest to 2008 (4–7 November 2005)

Polling question: 'Let me mention some people who might seek the Democratic nomination for president in 2008. If the next Democratic primary for president were being held today, for which one of the following candidates would you vote?'

Hillary Clinton	Senator (New York) and former First Lady
John Edwards	Former senator and 2004 vice-presidential candidate
Al Gore	Former vice-president and 2000 presidential candidate
John Kerry	Senator and 2004 presidential candidate
Joe Biden	Senator
Wesley Clark	Former US Army general and 2004 presidential hopeful
Bill Richardson	Governor (New Mexico)

Note: asked of registered voters who are Democrats, Democratic 'leaners', or are independents who would vote in a Democratic presidential primary.
Source: adapted from PollingReport.com (2005)

(a) Who appear to be front-runners and who can be described as 'no hopers'?

(b) Do the front-runners appear to share any common characteristics?

(c) Early polls generally provide a poor guide to the eventual winners of the party nominations. Why might this be?

Guidance

- The results of the polls that are conducted long before presidential election year are skewed by name recognition. Relatively well-known figures invariably score well. All the candidates named in the early polls for 2008 are former candidates or have been in the public eye for other reasons.

Task 1.1 (continued)

- In many earlier contests, the individual who seemed to be the front-runner 2 or 3 years before election year was swept aside as the contest drew closer. This is because individuals with name recognition are displaced by stronger candidates who were relatively unknown during the early stages of the contest. Table 1.1 shows the earlier front-runner who led the opinion polls and the eventual presidential candidate in a number of races for the Democratic Party's presidential nomination between 1976 and 2004.

Table 1.1 Democratic race — early front-runners and presidential candidates

Election year	Early front-runner	Background	Presidential candidate	Background
1976	Hubert Humphrey	Senator and vice-president, 1965–69	Jimmy Carter	Governor (Georgia)
1988	Gary Hart	Senator (and 1984 presidential contender)	Michael Dukakis	Governor (Colorado)
1992	Jerry Brown	Governor (California)	Bill Clinton	Governor (Arkansas)
2004	Richard Gephardt	House of Representatives (minority leader) and 1988 contender	John Kerry	Senator (Massachusetts)

Source: adapted from Cook (2003)

What is the role of formal and informal networks?

The building of informal, semi-formal and formal networks of supporters is critical. Their scale, and the degree to which they have a formal character, depends upon a candidate's resources, the scale of his or her ambitions, and the extent to which they can command support among party activists.

In early 2006, Senator Hillary Rodham Clinton had yet to announce her presidential intentions, and her public statements were instead concentrated on her re-election campaign in New York. Nonetheless, there were widely shared expectations that she would stand. As political analyst Walter Shapiro wrote in the online magazine *Salon* ('The Hillary juggernaut', www.salon.com/news/feature/2006/03/23/democrats/index_np.html), she 'hovers over the presidential field like the Statue of Liberty in New York harbor'.

Clinton's team was not only committed to the building of a fundraising machine but also sought to establish a national organisational structure to rival the Democratic National Committee which, under the chair of Howard Dean, the former Vermont governor who had sought the party's presidential nomination in 2004, was felt to be unpredictable. At the same time, as David Ignatius (2006) points out, Clinton's allies created the Center for American Progress to develop public policy ideas and proposals for reform.

How significant are straw polls?

The straw polls (or informal votes) that are organised as a test of opinion among party activists and supporters have no official status whatsoever. They are simply an informal measure of opinion among party supporters. Nonetheless, large sums are spent (in August 1999, Steve Forbes was said to have spent about $2 million), and the Ames straw poll has become increasingly important as a staging post on the road to the presidential nomination. As Dan Balz (1999) notes:

> When you get 25,000 or 30,000 people who give up a Saturday in August, hop on a bus and ride for an hour or two or more, not just for free food and entertainment, but to listen to their party's presidential candidates and show their support for them, that seems like a decent participatory event. When we decry the influence of television ads and the fact that so many people don't even bother to vote, it's good to see people getting directly involved — even if they were lured by the promise of free food and goody bags.

The 2006 Memphis straw poll

Although the 2008 presidential election was still $2\frac{1}{2}$ years away, *Hotline* (a newsletter) organised a straw poll at the Southern Republican Leadership Conference in March 2006; 1,427 votes were cast. There were few surprises about the winner: the Senate majority leader, Bill Frist, who represents Tennessee, attracted 37% of the vote. Although Senator John McCain was widely expected to be a strong contender in 2008, McCain urged those attending the conference not to back *him* but instead to show their support for the administration by writing in the name of George W. Bush on the ballot (10% of the votes went to Bush). Pundits suggested that McCain's move was designed to avert his

own defeat by Frist and win support among Bush loyalists. The long-term significance of the poll may, however, be the showing by Massachusetts governor Mitt Romney (14%) and Virginia senator George Allen (10%). As Chris Cilliza pointed out, the poll results enabled both to begin the process of establishing themselves as credible presidential candidates.

The 1999 Ames straw poll

Another Republican straw poll held during the summer of 1999 in the town of Ames, Iowa, was to play a significant role in the contest to win the 2000 presidential nomination. The gathering had a party atmosphere and candidates provided food and entertainment in a bid to attract supporters.

Table 1.2 Ames (Iowa) Republican straw poll, 2000

	Number of votes	% of poll	Background	Comments
George W. Bush	7,418	31	Texas governor	Elected president
Steve Forbes	4,921	21	Publisher	Withdrew in February 2000 after initial primaries
Elizabeth Dole	3,410	14	Former secretary of transportation	Withdrew 2 months later
Gary Bauer	2,114	9	Christian right organiser	Withdrew in February 2000 after initial primaries
Pat Buchanan	1,719	7	Presidential speechwriter and commentator	Later defected to the Reform Party
Lamar Alexander	1,428	6	Former Tennessee governor and Secretary of Education	Withdrew after Ames
Alan Keyes	1,101	5	Ambassador to UN	Withdrew in late July 2000
Dan Quayle	916	4	Former vice-president	Withdrew 1 month later
Orrin Hatch	558	2	Senator	Withdrew in January 2000
John McCain	83		Senator	Was not campaigning in Iowa — later won New Hampshire primary. Withdrew in March 2000

Table 1.2	continued

	Number of votes	% of poll	Background	Comments
John Kasich	9		Member of the House of Representatives	Withdrew 1 month before Ames
Bob Smith	8		Senator	Later defected to the US Constitution Party

Source: adapted from Yagielski and Hayden (1999)

Task 1.2

(a) To what extent do you think the 1999 Ames straw poll had an impact on the election process?

(b) Do straw polls add to, or detract from, the democratic process?

Guidance

- The Ames straw poll had a 'culling' function. George W. Bush's rejection of matching taxpayer funds (and the overall spending limits that acceptance imposed) played a role in dissuading former vice-president Dan Quayle, Elizabeth Dole and Lamar Alexander from pursuing their campaigns.
- Straw polls, and the festivities with which they are often associated, open up and extend the political process. They attract party supporters who might be reluctant to attend more formal meetings. At the same time, because such gatherings are open to more or less all comers, they are highly unrepresentative.

Box 1.2

Campaign strategists and advisors

The recruitment of well-known and experienced campaign strategists is important. In March 2006, Senator John McCain's prospects appeared to have been boosted when Terry Nelson, who had been national political director for President Bush's re-election race in 2004, became senior advisor to McCain's political action committee (Straight Talk America).

Cillizza and Goldfarb (2006)

Is fundraising critical?

A candidate's fundraising abilities are very important. Election campaigns are capital-intensive. The front-loading of the primaries and caucuses, so that a significant proportion are held during the first few weeks of the process, forces

candidates to campaign in a number of different states either at the same time or in quick succession. Older textbook notions that a relatively unknown candidate can secure support in the earlier contests and then accumulate the required funding and backing no longer apply. As Christopher Hanson (2003) notes, funding is required well before the first formal vote is cast:

> There was a time when a grass-roots candidate had a shot at raising sufficient cash after a strong showing in Iowa or New Hampshire to build significant momentum (George McGovern in 1972, Gary Hart in 1984). This was possible because the primary season was once three months long, stretching from March to June. That gave an underdog time to make the most of his victories, drawing press coverage, supporters, organizers, and donors between one election and the next.

> But since front loading took hold, there has not been enough time for an outsider to capitalize on an early win. The primaries are packed too tightly together for a poorly funded candidate to build real momentum. Thus in 1992, cash-strapped Democrat Paul Tsongas beat Bill Clinton in New Hampshire, only to be buried by Clinton money in the primary-crowded weeks that followed. In 1996 and 2000 the New Hampshire victors, Pat Buchanan and John McCain, met the same fate at the hands of the financial frontrunners, Bob Dole and George W. Bush.

Funding and political credibility

Financial resources are not only important for campaigning during the first few weeks of the primary season. They also serve another, earlier purpose: funds are seen as an indicator of a candidate's political credibility. In this way, they boost perceptions of a campaign's strength and resilience while at the same time deterring others from joining the contest. A particular candidate's funds can thereby 'thin out' the field of candidates at an early stage. For instance, in the run-up to the 2000 election, George W. Bush decided not to take the matching funds offered by the Federal Election Commission (FEC) (see Box 1.3) to primary candidates who can show a reasonably broad base of support and are willing to accept overall limits upon their campaign expenditure. Bush did this, in part, because Steve Forbes, another candidate in the race for the Republican presidential nomination, had also rejected FEC funding.

Bush's decision to cast off the restraints allowed him to raise and spend without limits. He raised nearly $40 million by mid-1999 and nearly $70 million by the end of 1999 (Cook 2003). The decision to reject public funding did not only permit Bush to counter the challenge posed by Forbes. It also contributed to the decision by other candidates such as Lamar Alexander, Elizabeth Dole and Dan Quayle to withdraw from the race. They were relatively well known but at that stage lacked the resources to fund themselves and would have been forced to mount limited campaigns had they accepted matching funds from the FEC.

> Box 1.3
> **What is the Federal Election Commission?**
>
> Public funding of both primaries and general elections was part of a package of reforms established under the 1971 Federal Election Campaign Act (FECA), which was then amended in 1974. Candidates who accept taxpayer funds must abide by the overall spending limits set by the Federal Election Commission. The funding system is not, however, compulsory. (This would almost certainly have been regarded by the courts as an infringement of an individual's First Amendment rights of both speech and assembly.)

Does the 'invisible primary' determine the eventual winner?

Most studies stress the key role played by opinion polls and the battle for funding in shaping the outcome of the invisible primary. William Schneider puts it in blunt terms: 'winning the invisible primary means two things: raising the most money, and becoming the front-runner in the polls' (2002, p. 24). As Table 1.3 shows, the front-runner who emerges from the 'invisible primary' often goes on to secure the party's presidential nomination.

Table 1.3　Early front-runners, 1980–2000

Election year	Party	Front-runner after the preceding mid-term elections	Party candidate
1980	Republican	Ronald Reagan	Ronald Reagan
1996	Republican	Bob Dole	Bob Dole
2000	Democrat	Al Gore	Al Gore
1988	Republican	George H. W. Bush	George H. W. Bush
2000	Republican	George W. Bush	George W. Bush

For his part, William Mayer points out that even the polls published just after the mid-term elections 2 years ahead of election day are a reliable guide to the eventual winner of the nomination:

> In seven of the last ten contested nomination races, the ultimate nominee, the eventual nominee, was the person who was leading the polls within a month after the preceding midterm election, so just about at this point in the nomination cycle…I characterize momentum as a bit like a roller-coaster ride. It provides a lot of excitement, a lot of

interesting moments. But, in the end, it pretty much takes you back to where you started off. And, so after all the forces of momentum have played out, the candidate who started out ahead almost always finishes ahead.

At first sight, the claim seems well founded. However, there have been some exceptions to the trend. Just after the 1978 mid-term contests, Senator Edward Kennedy was ahead of the incumbent president, Jimmy Carter, in the race for the Democratic nomination. After the 1990 mid-term elections, Mario Cuomo, the Governor of New York, led the Democratic pack, but later withdrew.

If, then, later poll ratings are taken and considered together with fundraising totals, they provide a more or less certain predictor of the outcome of the primary race. As Schneider records on the basis of Mayer's research:

> Does the invisible primary matter? You bet it does. Because nine times out of ten, whoever wins the invisible primary becomes the nominee…If one focuses on the last poll taken before the start of delegate selection activities — meaning, in most years, in the last poll before the Iowa caucuses — the candidate leading in that poll went on to win the nomination in nine out of 10 contests. The exception: Gary Hart was the Democratic front-runner just before the 1988 Iowa caucuses…The leading money-raiser in the pre-primary campaign — more precisely, the candidate who had raised the largest amount of money by December 31 of the year before the election — went on to win the nomination nine out of 10 times. The exception: John Connally had raised more money than Ronald Reagan by December 31, 1979.

Table 1.4 considers a broader range of contests than Table 1.3. It shows that, although there are some important exceptions, the 'winner' of at least one of the key components of the 'invisible primary' has gone on to win the party nomination.

| Table 1.4 | Fundraising leaders, poll ratings and the presidential candidate, 1980–2004 |

Election year	Party	Presidential candidate	Fundraising leader (at the end of the pre-election year)	Gallup poll leader (at the beginning of election year)
2004	D	John Kerry	Howard Dean	Howard Dean
2000	D	Al Gore	Al Gore	Al Gore
	R	George W. Bush	George W. Bush	George W. Bush
1996	R	Bob Dole	Bob Dole	Bob Dole
1992	D	Bill Clinton	Bill Clinton	Jerry Brown
	R	George H. W. Bush	George H. W. Bush	George H. W. Bush
1988	D	Michael Dukakis	Michael Dukakis	Gary Hart
	R	George H. W. Bush	George H. W. Bush	George H. W. Bush
1984	D	Walter Mondale	Walter Mondale	Walter Mondale

Table
1.4 continued

Election year	Party	Presidential candidate	Fundraising leader (at the end of the pre-election year)	Gallup poll leader (at the beginning of election year)
1980	D	Jimmy Carter	Jimmy Carter	Jimmy Carter
1980	R	Ronald Reagan	John Connally	Ronald Reagan

Note: the table does not include incumbent presidents seeking re-election who have faced credible opposition from within their own party. Source: Cohen et al. (2003)

How important are key party members?

There is, however, another perspective. Despite the stress that is customarily placed upon the opinion polls and fundraising totals, others emphasise the role of leading party figures (such as governors and members of Congress) in shaping the outcome of the invisible primary. From this perspective, other components of the invisible primary, such as a candidate's financial 'war chest' and his or her position in the opinion polls undoubtedly matter, but they are secondary. A study by the Brookings Institution, an influential Washington-based think-tank, suggested that George W. Bush emerged as the front-runner in the race for the Republican presidential nomination during the 'invisible primary' that preceded the 2000 election because he had the backing of influential Republican insiders. His principal rival, Senator John McCain, was widely regarded as a maverick. In the 2000 contest, other early candidates (such as Steve Forbes) were well funded but their campaigns failed to gain momentum. As the Brookings study concluded:

> What, then, was driving his candidacy — the judgment of insiders that he would make a strong candidate or the polls? On the basis of the statistical analysis reported earlier, we can say that if Republican insiders had massed behind Elizabeth Dole or especially John McCain, Bush would probably not have won his party's nomination — or perhaps even entered the race.
>
> William Schneider (2002)

Does success at the invisible primary always guarantee success?

No. There have been times when success at the invisible primary has not meant a successful nomination. One such example is Howard Dean: by the end of 2003, former governor of Vermont Howard Dean appeared assured of the

Democrats' 2004 presidential nomination. His campaign had a 'grassroots' character. It made imaginative use of the internet using campaign blogs to build a sense of involvement, conducting online polls on particular issues, and making appeals for campaign contributions. By the end of September 2003, the Dean campaign had raised $25.4 million (although George Bush had by then collected $84.6 million). Most of this was from large numbers of small-scale donors. Like a number of other candidates (including Bush) Dean decided, after an online vote, not to accept matching taxpayer funding and his campaign was not therefore bound by overall spending limits. During the later stages of the 'invisible primary', Dean also gained endorsements from significant numbers of trade unions and influential figures within the Democratic Party. Their ranks included former vice-president, Al Gore.

However, although Dean 'won' the 'invisible primary', his campaign quickly imploded. He slipped in the final polls and then finished third in the Iowa caucuses. Senator John Kerry was victorious, providing him with the momentum to win most of the subsequent contests and secure the nomination without difficulty.

In the wake of his Iowa defeat, Dean's attempts to rally supporters through an emotional speech ending in what became known as the 'Dean scream' were mocked widely on nationwide television. He came a distant second in the New Hampshire primary. He only won his home state of Vermont and was forced to withdraw. As the New Hampshire newspaper, *Union Leader*, noted in an editorial:

> Back when Mr Dean had ridiculous leads in the polls, Mr Kerry often ranked as respondents' second choice. It was indeed as if voters 'dated Dean, but married Kerry'...Mr Dean was a romantic figure, saying all the right things and sweeping people off their feet. But the hotter the romance, the shorter-lived. [Tuesday's] results confirm the image of Mr Kerry as the stable provider. He may be boring...but more Democrats have decided that he's the one who can bring home the bacon, which in this case is the White House.
>
> From *Union Leader*, quoted in *Guardian*, 29 January (2004)

Task 1.3

(a) What conclusions should be drawn from Howard Dean's rise and fall?

(b) What factors shape the outcome of the 'invisible primary'?

(c) Evaluate the accuracy of the 'invisible primary' in 'predicting' the outcome of the party nomination races.

Task 1.3 (continued)

Guidance

You might consider the following points:

- Does Howard Dean's fate suggest that the 'invisible primary' is rather less important than had hitherto been assumed? Or was it simply a special case?
- The 'invisible primary' has often 'predicted' the outcome of the nomination race with accuracy. Indeed, up until 2004, it was a more reliable guide to the winner than the Iowa and New Hampshire contests.
- There is a debate about the character of the 'invisible primary'. Whereas some stress the part played by the opinion polls and funding totals, others emphasise the role of party elites in determining the eventual outcome.
- Fundraising almost always seems to be the key indicator. In nine of the ten contested nominating battles between 1980 and 2000, the fundraising leader in the year prior to the election has gone on to win the nomination. Over the same period, candidates who have been the leading preference of their party's voters in the first Gallup Poll of the presidential election year have captured the nomination eight times.
- The year 2004 proved exceptional. Despite widespread expectations that Howard Dean would capture the Democratic nomination, his campaign imploded as soon as the first caucuses and primaries were held.

Further reading and references

- Balz, D. (1999) 'The Iowa straw poll', *The Washington Post*, 16 August.
- Cillizza, C. 'Frist wins, Romney runs strong second', *The Washington Post* website.
- Cillizza, C. and Goldfarb, Z. A. (2006) 'McCain campaign hires "best bricklayer"', *The Washington Post*, 19 March.
- CNN (2002) 'Bush names Stephen Friedman Chief Economic Adviser; Trent Lott still under fire for comments at Thurmond celebration', 12 December.
- Cohen, M., Karol, D., Noel, H. and Zaller, J. (2003) 'Polls or pols? The real driving force behind presidential nominations', *The Brookings Review*, vol. 21, no. 3, pp. 36- 39.
- Cook, R. (2003) *Winning 'the Invisible Primary'*, www.rhodescook.com/winning.html
- Federal Election Commission (2004) *Presidential Pre-Nomination Campaign Receipts Through December 31, 2003.*
- *Guardian* (2004) 'They dated Dean, but married Kerry: New Hampshire voters have chosen John Kerry', 29 January.

Chapter 1

- Hanson, C. (2003) 'Voices: the invisible primary. Now is the time for all-out coverage', *Columbia Journalism Review*, March/April, www.cjr.org/issues/2003/2/voices-hanson.asp
- Ignatius, D. (2006) 'A party waiting to pounce', *The Washington Post*, 29 March.
- PollingReport.com (2005) *Election 2008.*
- Schneider, W. (2002) 'Let the "Invisible Primary" begin', *The Atlantic*, 24 December.
- Yagielski, J. and Hayden, K. (1999) 'Bush wins Iowa GOP straw poll', CNN/AllPolitics, 15 August, http://cnn.com

Chapter 2

Should the pre-nomination system be reformed?

Chapter 2 considers the first few months of presidential election year. Although the US system of choosing party candidates is much more open than that in many other countries, it has also been subject to criticism. This chapter therefore assesses the case for reform.

The first few months of presidential election year are dominated by the primaries and caucuses. In contrast with the 'invisible primary', which rests on the outcome of opinion polls, popular expectations, media representations, fundraising and the judgements of party elites, the primaries and caucuses involve 'real' votes. As you will discover, there are significant differences between states and some differences between the parties.

What is the role of the primaries and caucuses?

Although there are different rules and procedures in each state, primaries and caucuses allow registered party supporters to play a part in deciding on their party's candidate.

Task 2.1

Read this quotation from James Davis and answer the questions that follow.

> The process of national leadership recruitment in the United States is governed by an imposing mixture of party rules and federal and state laws that present a formidable challenge to any aspiring presidential contender.
>
> Party rules, especially in the Democratic Party, spell out how many delegates each state will be allocated and how the delegates are to be apportioned on

Task 2.1 (continued)

the basis of primary election or caucus-convention results, require equal representation of men and women on all national convention delegations, and determine how many uncommitted national convention delegate slots for party official ('superdelegates') will be authorized. State law determines whether a state will use a presidential primary, caucus-convention system, a state party committee, or a combination of the latter two to select national convention delegates. State legislatures establish dates on which the primary or caucus will be held, the filing deadlines for candidates in the primaries, how many signatures are required on petitions for ballot access, and so on.

Davis (1997), p. 3

(a) What are 'superdelegates'?

(b) What is a 'caucus-convention system'?

(c) Why is the Democratic Party more committed to rules restricting the choice of national convention delegates?

(d) The author refers to the role of federal and state law, as well as party rules, in determining the character of 'national leadership recruitment'. In what ways does federal and state law shape the process?

Guidance

- 'Superdelegates' are Democratic Party officials who have an assigned place at national conventions. They include members of the Democratic National Committee, senators and members of the House of Representatives, state governors and 'distinguished party leaders' such as former presidents and vice-presidents.

- The 'superdelegate' system was established as a reaction to the grassroots-based convention delegate system that the Democrats had adopted following the report of the McGovern–Fraser commission (1970). It was hoped that the presence of 'superdelegates' would introduce a degree of peer review into the presidential candidate selection process. It was felt that this had been absent in 1972 when the Democrats picked Senator George McGovern, a relatively radical candidate, as the presidential nominee.

- In 2004, there were 802 'superdelegates' at the Democratic convention in Boston. Despite initial appearances, they are not insulated from the ebbs and flows of the political process. Indeed, even before the primaries begin, they are subject to lobbying by campaigns seeking to maximise their delegate count. CNN recorded that John Edwards' campaign began to track superdelegates in December 2003 and intensified its efforts in February 2004. For its part, the Kerry campaign ensured that the superdelegates who had by that stage been named received regular telephone calls and e-mails from campaign staff members or the candidate himself.

- Most states hold primaries during the early months of election year. (These are conventional elections. Voting is usually, but not always, limited to registered party

Task 2.1 (continued)

supporters.) Some states, however, hold caucuses (although there may be variations in the form that these take). This is sometimes dubbed the 'caucus-convention' system.

> ...the modern caucus system is similar to a primary in that all party members within the state are eligible to participate. In Iowa...the 2,500 precinct caucuses are convened each four years on a frosty winter evening in local homes, schools, fire stations, and even local barbershops.
>
> Davis (1997), p. 45

The function of caucuses

Precinct caucuses, or neighbourhood meetings, choose delegates who later attend county conventions. They will be pledged to back a particular candidate on the basis of voting at the caucuses (see Box 2.1). This is called 'delegate apportionment'. The caucuses may also pass resolutions addressing policy issues. The county conventions are generally held a few months later in April or May. These select a rather smaller number of delegates who will attend Congressional District caucuses or conventions. (A Congressional District is an area represented by one member of the US House of Representatives.) These delegates are chosen so as to reflect the vote for presidential candidates at the precinct caucuses. The Congressional District caucuses or conventions choose the delegates who will attend the national convention. They also send delegates to the party's state convention. This chooses 'at-large' convention delegates who serve on behalf of the entire state party rather than a particular Congressional District. Although

Box 2.1

Caucuses

Caucuses are meetings. They offer an opportunity to discuss the strengths and weaknesses of the different candidates before votes are taken. The caucuses generally choose delegates who attend county and state conventions, which, in turn, select delegates who will be sent to the party's national convention during the summer months. The caucus system is complex and attendance may often be confined to strong party identifiers who can withstand the rigours of a lengthy meeting.

There are both open and closed primaries. The system is determined by state law and party rules. In closed primaries, voting is restricted to those who registered as party supporters at an earlier stage. Open primaries allow same-day party registration or, in some instances, allow independents or even supporters of another party, to vote.

A caucus meeting in progress

federal law establishes voting rights, state law regulates most election procedures and the form of election that is used.

> Functioning under different rules and requiring different campaign strategies, national convention delegate hunting in the caucus states is, in many respects, more complicated and time consuming for the presidential candidates than primary campaigning. Electoral success in the caucus-convention state, most analysts agree, turns less on general popularity and media campaigning and far more on a strong, well-financed campaign organization. Indeed, the key to success is to round up as many identified supporters and get them to attend the precinct caucuses.
>
> Davis (1997), p. 49

Equality of outcome

The Democratic Party is more ideologically committed to ensuring that women and minorities are fully represented. This is sometimes called 'equality of outcome'. The party has therefore adopted formal procedures to try to ensure this. Its rules include provisions that women should constitute half the convention delegates.

To what extent do Iowa and New Hampshire set the pace?

The first 'real' votes in the party nomination battles are, by tradition, held in Iowa and New Hampshire, although other states have sometimes sought to 'leapfrog' these contests by holding their primaries some days earlier. These efforts, however, are unrecognised by the parties and do not have official status.

Table 2.1 shows that Iowa and New Hampshire play a pivotal role in the candidate selection process. They set the pace and frame the character of the race, which shapes the later contests. A candidate almost always has to win at least one of these states. Only Bill Clinton failed to win either state, although he was depicted as a 'winner' in New Hampshire because his vote exceeded expectations.

Table 2.1 Iowa, New Hampshire and the party nomination

Year	Party	Iowa winner	New Hampshire winner	Presidential candidate
1980	Republicans	George H. W. Bush	Ronald Reagan	Ronald Reagan
1980	Democrats	Jimmy Carter*	Jimmy Carter*	Jimmy Carter
1984	Republicans	Ronald Reagan*	Ronald Reagan*	Ronald Reagan*
1984	Democrats	Walter Mondale	Gary W. Hart	Walter Mondale
1988	Republicans	Bob Dole	George H. W. Bush	George H. W. Bush
1988	Democrats	Richard Gephardt	Michael Dukakis	Michael Dukakis
1992	Republicans	George H. W. Bush*	George H. W. Bush	George H. W. Bush*
1992	Democrats	Tom Harkin	Paul E. Tsongas	Bill Clinton
1996	Republicans	Bob Dole	Patrick J. Buchanan	Bob Dole
1996	Democrats	Bill Clinton*	Bill Clinton*	Bill Clinton*
2000	Republicans	George W. Bush	John McCain	George W. Bush
2000	Democrats	Al Gore	Al Gore	Al Gore
2004	Republicans	George W. Bush*	George W. Bush*	George W. Bush*
2004	Democrats	John Kerry	John Kerry	John Kerry

Note: an asterisk denotes an incumbent president. In most cases, the re-nomination of an incumbent president is a formality. However, Jimmy Carter faced a serious and sustained challenge from Senator Edward Kennedy in 1980. In 1992, the maverick right-winger, Patrick J. Buchanan (who won the New Hampshire primary in 1996) stood against President George H. W. Bush. He did not win a single contest but gained 37% of the vote in New Hampshire. This was widely seen as damaging and may have contributed to Bush's loss of the White House later in the year.

Although Iowa and New Hampshire have an almost mythic significance in the US presidential election calendar, the results of the Iowa caucuses and the New Hampshire primary have often been idiosyncratic. If incumbent presidents seeking re-election are disregarded (because the contest is almost always a mere formality), the victors in these early states have often disappeared from sight within days of the vote. In 1992, Bill Clinton was defeated in both Iowa and New Hampshire. However, once the New Hampshire result was announced, his second place allowed him to claim to be the 'comeback kid' and he went on to win subsequent primaries, secure the Democratic nomination and take the presidency.

However, the 2004 contests in Iowa and New Hampshire had a particular significance because they dashed Howard Dean's hopes of winning the nomination and quickly established John Kerry as front-runner.

Table 2.2 Democratic contest, Iowa caucuses, 19 January 2004

Candidate	Background	Percentage of the vote
John Kerry	Massachusetts senator	38
John Edwards	North Carolina senator	32
Howard Dean	Former Vermont governor	18
Richard Gephardt	Former House minority leader	11
Dennis Kucinich	Member (House of Representatives)	1
Al Sharpton	Preacher	0

Note: other candidates including Carol Moseley Braun were listed but had, by then, withdrawn from the contest.
Source: adapted from CNN.com

Table 2.3 New Hampshire primary, 27 January 2004

Candidate	Percentage of vote
John Kerry	39
Howard Dean	26
Wesley Clark	13
John Edwards	12
Joseph Lieberman	9
Dennis Kucinich	1
Al Sharpton	0

Source: adapted from CNN.com

Are Iowa and New Hampshire still relevant?

The Iowa caucuses and the New Hampshire traditionally played a pivotal role. However, recent studies have tended instead to stress the importance of the 'invisible primary' in determining the final outcome. The 2004 Democratic nomination contest changed this. Iowa and New Hampshire acquired fresh importance.

The prospect of Dean being selected as the Democrats' 2004 presidential candidate had led to jubilation among Republican strategists. They believed that he would be seen by the wider voting public as a radical and that George W. Bush would win a landslide re-election victory. Some drew comparisons with 1972 when the Democrats selected George McGovern, who campaigned on a liberal platform. The incumbent Republican president, Richard Nixon, was re-elected overwhelmingly.

At the time when Dean appeared to be heading towards victory, the other candidates in the race for the Democratic nomination seemed to be in trouble. They were not only behind in the polls but had serious difficulties raising the requisite funds. Two of the better-known Democratic contenders, General Wesley Clark and Senator Joseph Lieberman (who had served as vice-presidential candidate in 2000), therefore decided not to stand in Iowa but concentrate instead on winning in New Hampshire. Past experience suggested that Iowa was not critical. For his part, Senator John Kerry took a different decision. Despite financial pressures, he threw all his resources into Iowa and devoted little time or attention to New Hampshire. It was a high-risk strategy. If the bid to win Iowa had failed there would have been no way of continuing the campaign.

However, Kerry's gamble paid off. There was a shift to Kerry as grassroots party supporters began to accept that he was — as a long-serving senator with a distinguished Vietnam war record — a far more credible presidential candidate. As one observer put it, Democrats 'dated' Dean but 'married' Kerry.

Kerry's victory in Iowa enabled him to build up momentum in New Hampshire within just a few days. Clark and Lieberman could not match this and both withdrew from the presidential race at an early stage. Having won both the Iowa and New Hampshire contests, Kerry went on to win almost all the later primaries and secure the nomination.

Task 2.2

To what extent do the Iowa caucuses and the New Hampshire primary 'pick' the eventual winner of the party nomination?

Guidance

- Although included in Table 2.1, incumbent presidents are special cases. Some have faced credible — or at least sustained — challenges. In 1980, Jimmy Carter was challenged by Senator Edward Kennedy. In 1992, George H. W. Bush faced Patrick J. Buchanan in New Hampshire. However, they are generally unopposed within their own party or at the least encounter no serious opposition.

- Up until 2004, most observers stressed the role of the 'invisible primary' and argued that Iowa and New Hampshire played a lesser role. Often, they noted, maverick candidates (most notably Patrick J. Buchanan) had won in either Iowa or New Hampshire but it made little long-term difference to the contest. Other candidates established themselves in the later primaries, particularly on 'Super Tuesday', when a significant number of states — particularly southern states — vote on the same day.

- The 2004 experience may lead to a re-evaluation. Although Howard Dean undoubtedly 'won' the 'invisible primary' and many observers believed that the primary season would be almost a formality, his campaign collapsed as the Iowa caucuses drew near. Iowa was also crucial for John Kerry. His success in Iowa created a sense of momentum that enabled him to win in New Hampshire and nearly all the later primaries.

Should Iowa and New Hampshire maintain their place in the primary calendar?

Questions have been asked about the extent to which Iowa and New Hampshire are representative of the American nation. Nelson Polsby, the Heller Professor of Political Science at the University of California, asked: 'Why should a tiny New Hampshire with its elderly population, its large French-speaking minority, its backward economy, and its lack of state-wide communication other than the wildly idiosyncratic *Manchester Union-Leader* have such influence?'

Task 2.3

Examine Table 2.4 and answer the questions that follow.

Table 2.4 Iowa, New Hampshire and the USA, character and composition

	Iowa	New Hampshire	USA
Population (2004, estimate)	2,954,451	1,299,500	293,655,404
Population, percentage change, 1990–2000	5.4	11.4	13.1
Population, percentage change, 1 April 2000–1 July 2004	1.0	5.2	4.3
Persons under 18 years old (%), 2000	25.1	25.0	25.7
Persons per household, 2000	2.46	2.53	2.59
Persons 65 years old and over (%), 2000	14.9	12.0	12.4
Median household income, 1999	$39,469	$49,467	$41,994
Bachelor's degree or higher (% of persons aged 25+), 2000	21.2	28.7	24.4
White persons (%), 2000	93.9	96.0	75.1
Black or African-American persons (%), 2000	2.1	0.7	12.3
Foreign-born persons (%), 2000	3.1	4.4	11.1
Minority-owned firms (% of total), 1997	2.3	2.8	14.6
Persons below poverty line (%), 1999	9.1	6.5	12.4

Source: adapted from US Census Bureau (2005)

(a) How representative, or unrepresentative, are Iowa and New Hampshire?

(b) Do you consider Polsby's comments fair?

Guidance

You might consider the following points in your answer:
● The relative size and racial/ethnic composition of the states have often provoked attention insofar as both Iowa and New Hampshire are overwhelmingly white.

Task 2.3 (continued)

Nonetheless, median household income in Iowa and New Hampshire is close to the national figure.

- The age structure of Iowa and New Hampshire does not differ significantly from the national age structure. Polsby's comments also raise a question: can any state be considered 'representative'?

What is the role of the South Carolina primary?

The South Carolina primary has acquired growing significance in Republican contests. In 2000, Senator John McCain had been victorious in New Hampshire and posed a serious threat to George W. Bush's bid to win the Republican nomination. Because of this threat, the South Carolina contest, on 19 February, acquired much greater significance.

South Carolina is, like many of the other southern states, relatively conservative. As you will see from Table 2.5, evangelical Christians, who are strongly committed to family values and moral traditionalism, are well represented here. They oppose abortion and moves towards same-sex marriage. They strongly support school prayer.

Table 2.5 Proportion of evangelicals participating in Republican primaries

New Hampshire	South Carolina	Michigan	Virginia	New York
16	34	27	19	15

Source: adapted from White (2003) and *The New York Times*/CBS News (2004)

Table 2.6 indicates the share of the votes gained by Republicans in South Carolina.

Table 2.6 South Carolina primary (Republican), 2000 — share of the vote gained by the principal candidates

Candidate	Share of vote (%)
George W. Bush	53.39
John McCain	41.87
Alan Keyes	4.54
Gary Bauer	0.11
Steve Forbes	0.08

Source: adapted from Federal Election Commission (2000)

Task 2.4

Critics of the primary system argue that it assigns a disproportionate role to Iowa, New Hampshire and — among Republicans — South Carolina, which, they argue, are unrepresentative states. Do you consider this a fair comment?

Guidance

- South Carolina has a high proportion of evangelical 'born-again' Christians, many of whom are deeply conservative. Most back the Republican Party, and according to some observers they play a disproportionate role — through their votes in the South Carolina — in determining the outcome of the Republican presidential nomination race. Others, however, point out that in 2000, South Carolina had a 'modified open primary' system that allowed independents to vote. The McCain campaign was initially hopeful that he could win their backing enabling him to defeat Bush. However, Bush had strong backing from leaders of the Christian right and this enabled his campaign to mobilise substantial numbers of evangelicals. His victory was a major setback for McCain and set the Bush campaign on the road to victory. In early March, McCain formally withdrew from the contest and endorsed Bush.
- Iowa and New Hampshire are relatively small states with a largely rural character, but they are not the backwaters that some commentaries suggest. The proportion of young people is close to the national average and New Hampshire has experienced significant population growth in recent years. Nonetheless, both states are overwhelmingly white and do not suffer from the poverty levels that can be found in other areas of the USA.

Why is turnout for the primaries so low?

Primaries have been criticised because of their low turnout: relatively small numbers of voters participate. There are suggestions, furthermore, that primaries and caucuses contribute to 'voter fatigue'. From this perspective, there are so many opportunities to vote — at local, state and national level and in referendums — that this leads to boredom with the political process and thereby depresses turnout.

Task 2.5

On the basis of the figures in Table 2.7 and other information in this chapter, explain why turnout is often so low in the primaries and caucuses.

Task 2.5 (continued)

Table 2.7 Turnout in 2004 and 2000 for selected primaries/caucuses

State/jurisdiction	2004 (% of VEP)	2000 (% of VEP)
Iowa	6.1	6.8
New Hampshire	29.9	44.4
Arizona	6.5	12.7
Delaware	5.6	7.6
Missouri	12.9	18.6
Tennessee	10.9	11.3
Wisconsin	24.6	22.7
California	31.0	n/a
Connecticut	5.7	15.6
Georgia	13.5	17.7
Maryland	16.6	25.2
Massachusetts	15.1	n/a

Note: the VEP is the voter eligible population. This is a smaller number than the voting age population (VAP) that is more usually cited in turnout estimates. The VEP excludes resident aliens, convicted felons and others who do not have the right to vote. It is therefore a more useful starting point for calculations.
Source: adapted from United States Elections Project (2004)

Guidance

- Turnout is relatively low in all US elections. This may be attributable to 'voter fatigue'.
- The later primaries tend to be uncompetitive. Usually, one candidate has established a clear lead within the first few weeks. Other candidates then have difficulty attracting funds and are often compelled to drop out. Only candidates with a radical platform carry on beyond this point. If an election is uncompetitive, lower numbers are likely to cast a vote.
- Caucuses are meetings that often take many hours. There is discussion about the strengths of the different candidates and votes are then tallied. As a result, these procedures tend to attract those who are most committed to particular candidates and discourage others.

How representative is the primary electorate?

The debate over the character of the primary electorate is not confined to a discussion of Iowa, New Hampshire and South Carolina. Because overall turnout levels are low, there has also been controversy about the nature of all those who vote during the primary season.

Task 2.6

Read the six different perspectives on how representative the primary electorate is and answer the questions that follow:

(1) Morris P. Fiorina suggests that the growth of primaries and caucuses has, together with other developments, allowed 'the ascendance of the purists'. The selection process attracts the most politically committed activists. They are driven by ideological zeal:

> Such individuals are dedicated, committed to winning, and hostile towards compromise. They are important to candidates as financial donors and disproportionately represented in press and television news reports. At the same time, new opportunities for political participation have opened up with both the growth of government responsibilities, the dramatic expansion of interest group activity, and the demise of the party 'bosses' who once dominated the candidate selection process.
>
> Fiorina et al. (2005), pp. 144–45

(2) Nonetheless, there do appear to be demographic differences between the primary electorate and the general population. In a 1972 article, Austin Ranney noted that:

> ...presidential primary electorates, like those in gubernatorial primaries, are demographically quite unrepresentative of the nonparticipating party identi-fiers: they are older, of higher status in income and occupation, and more active in a variety of civic, religious, and political organizations.
>
> Quoted in Davis (1997), p. 183

(3) Austin Ranney also argued that strong partisans were 'only slightly more likely' to vote in the presidential primaries' (quoted in Davis 1997, p. 183).

(4) In a more recent survey of Republican primary voters, Barbara Norrander suggests that there are relatively few differences between those who participate in primaries and those who, later in the year, vote in the general election.

> ...Republican primary voters may be slightly more ideologically sophisticated (e.g. more ideologues) and have somewhat stronger symbolic ideological identifications...but they are not more ideologically extreme...Primary voters are not the extremist minority; they are the slightly better informed minority.
>
> Norrander (1996), p. 888

(5) A distinction should, however, be drawn between primaries and caucuses. The system of caucuses held in some states offers particular opportunities for activist participation. A 1988 study of Iowa, Michigan and Virginia by William G. Mayer found that caucus participants differ markedly from the general population in

Task 2.6 (continued)

terms of education, age, income and rates of party activity. The study also concluded that 'caucus participants in both parties do have a pronounced ideological tilt to them, far more so than primary voters or party identifiers' (quoted in Davis 1997, p. 182). Republican participants were more likely than Republican voters and identifiers to define themselves as 'conservative', while Democratic participants were more likely to see themselves as 'liberal'.

(6) Caucuses are generally tied to the holding of a subsequent state party convention that formally selects the presidential candidate and shapes the policy positions that will be taken by the state party's national convention delegates. As Rozell and Wilcox record, the state-wide Republican convention in Virginia is open to any citizen who is willing to pledge support to the party's nominees. The Christian right has just to muster a few thousand delegates and it can wield significant influence. As Ralph Reed, former executive director of the Christian Coalition, noted in 1994:

> ...the caucus-convention process in the [Virginia] Republican Party is unusual in that it does tend to give [our] grassroots activists a greater voice than they have in primaries...
>
> Quoted in Rozell and Wilcox (2003), p. 42

Virginia is not alone. As Lamare, Polinard, and Wrinkle record, the Texas Christian Coalition has played a major role in the Republican precinct conventions that are held at the conclusion of primary election day. They choose delegates for the county conventions which in turn select the state convention delegates. By 1994, the activism of the Coalition had paid off. Over 60% of the delegates and alternates who attended the state party convention were 'social conservatives' (Lamare et al. 2003, p. 69).

(a) In what ways do the perspectives offered by Morris Fiorina and Austin Ranney differ from the commentaries in (3) and (4)?

(b) What conclusions should be drawn from extracts (5) and (6)?

Guidance

- Whereas many other commentaries suggest that the electorate in the primaries is broadly representative of the US voter, Austin Ranney and Morris Fiorina stress its unrepresentative character. Ranney points to demographic variables while Fiorina asserts that the caucuses are dominated by 'purists'. He is referring to the activists who are driven by ideological commitment and zeal.
- There is a significant difference between primaries and caucuses. The caucuses attract the more committed party identifiers, and the county/state conventions, to which they are tied, offer opportunities to particular cause groups and those who others might define as 'extremists'.

Chapter 2

What are the consequences of 'front-loading'?

> The front-runner apparently will have up to $100 million to spend in the Republican primary. And after New Hampshire — this is a very important point, and it was very critical in my decision — there will be 18 primaries within 30 days of the New Hampshire primary. If I would win the New Hampshire primary, which I think I had a reasonable chance of doing, looking at the amount of money that I would have to raise and the calendar of these primaries, it became a very difficult proposition. There would be little time for reflection on what we had just achieved. There would not be sufficient time to raise the resources to be competitive in states like California, New York, Ohio, Michigan — major expensive states. And so, reality set in.
>
> Former vice-president Dan Quayle (1999)

The primaries have been criticised for being 'front-loaded'. This means that the dates on which a significant number of primaries are held are bunched together at the beginning of the cycle. This prevents an 'outsider' candidate establishing him or herself in the early primaries and then building up support and financial backing during the later primaries. This, it is said, gives an unfair advantage to well-known candidates who have extensive resources and well-established national campaigns.

Despite these criticisms, states and state parties are often anxious to hold their primary or caucus at an early stage to ensure that their voters have an effective say in deciding the parties' presidential candidates. This has led to the creation of 'Junior Tuesday', when the New England states come together to gain leverage and establish a counterweight to the influence of the southern states. At the same time, influential candidates may seek to have the date of a particular primary moved forwards if they expect to do well. (There were suggestions that in 1992, Bill Clinton persuaded the state governor, Zell Miller, to move the Georgia primary forward a week to help his bid for the nomination.) Furthermore, the Republican Party uses a 'winner-takes-all' system of delegate allocation to a greater extent, so that if a candidate wins a state's primary, all or most of that state's national convention delegates — during the summer months — make the formal decision about the nominee. The Democrats use a more proportionate system. A Republican candidate can therefore gain a winning majority of delegates at an earlier stage.

The drift towards front-loading has continued. Indeed, some suggest that as the primary season becomes ever more compressed, the USA is moving towards a *de facto* national primary in which all states hold their contests at about the same time.

| Table 2.8 | Dates of key primaries, 2000 and 2004 |

2004 date	State	2000 date
13 January	District of Columbia	2 May
3 February	Arizona	22 February (D) and 7 March (R)
3 February	New Mexico	6 June
3 February	Missouri	7 March
3 February	South Carolina	19 February (R) and 9 March (D)
3 February	Oklahoma	14 March
7 February	Michigan	22 February (R) and 11 March (D)
7 February	Washington	29 February
10 February	Virginia	29 February (R) and 3 June (D)
10 February	Tennessee	14 March
17 February	Wisconsin	4 April
24 February	Idaho	23 May
24 February	Utah	10 March

Task 2.7

(a) Why is the primary system becoming more 'front-loaded'?

(b) What are the consequences of 'front-loading'?

Guidance

• The reasons for the drift towards 'front-loading' include jostling among the states and state parties, many of which hope to play a part in determining the outcome of the contest.

• Most observers are highly critical of 'front-loading'. It discriminates, they argue, against candidates with limited resources. It therefore makes the primaries less open to outsider candidates. Nonetheless, 'front-loading' may have advantages. A much shorter primary season would take less of a toll on candidates. It would give more weight to the larger states and, correspondingly, unrepresentative states such as Iowa and New Hampshire would play less of a role.

Should the early primaries be reformed?

In March 2006, the Democratic National Committee's Rules and Bylaws Committee considered a plan put forward by the party's Commission on

Presidential Nomination Timing and Scheduling to allow other states, apart from Iowa and New Hampshire, to hold early primaries and caucuses. Iowa and New Hampshire would retain their traditional places as the first in the primary calendar. However, up to two states would be allowed to hold caucuses after Iowa but before New Hampshire. Furthermore, one or two other states would be permitted to hold primaries after New Hampshire but before 5 February, the formal start date for the remainder of the nation. These would be states, according to the plan's supporters, that were relatively small, thereby allowing credible campaigns by candidates with only limited resources, but would be those that were more socially diverse than Iowa and New Hampshire. According to a spokesperson for Senator John Edwards, the former North Carolina senator who was the Democrats' vice-presidential running mate in 2004, there would be 'some additional geographic, racial and economic diversity in the early voting' (Cillizza and Moreno 2006).

At the same time, the committee sought to allay fears that this would make the process more 'front-loaded' insofar as many of the primaries are bunched together in the early weeks of the primary season. It considered the use of 'bonus' national convention delegates to reward states that were prepared to hold their contests later in the season (Toner 2006).

Task 2.8

The reform proposals were opposed by the New Hampshire governor (a Democrat) and at least one of those considered to be a 2008 presidential contender, Senator Evan Bayh of Indiana. What do you think are the arguments *against* their adoption?

Guidance

Although the plan might reduce the overall importance of the Iowa caucuses and the New Hampshire primary, and the other early primaries would be held in small states, there would be further 'front-loading' adding to the demands (in terms of both funds and human resources) imposed upon candidates. There is also the argument that because Iowa and New Hampshire are among the less populous states, but at the same time the campaigns require hard, competitive campaigning, candidates are compelled to meet individual voters, talk to them (sometimes in their homes) and engage in serious persuasion. A spokesman for Senator Evan Bayh said that 'we need places…where the voters get to meet the candidates one-on-one…Someplace where it isn't all about who has the most money or the best TV ad' (Cillizza and Moreno 2006).

What tactics and strategies do candidates adopt during the primary season?

The tactics adopted by a candidate will depend in part upon the political character of his or her campaign (see Box 2.2). Moderate Republicans such as Senator John McCain (who stood in 2000) have tended to concentrate their resources in states holding open primaries. These allow independents and in some cases supporters of the opposing party to cast a vote or permit same-day registration. In 2000, McCain's backing in Michigan and (in the Democratic race) John Edwards' support in Wisconsin are partly attributable to 'cross-over' voting by non-Republicans.

Box 2.2

Examples of tactics

- 'Stop lying about my record' (Senator Bob Dole to Vice-President George H. W. Bush during the 1988 Republican primary race).
- On the eve of the 1992 New Hampshire primary, Governor Bill Clinton authorised the execution of a mentally retarded man. This, critics suggested, confirmed his law-and-order credentials. According to journalist Christopher Hitchens: 'The lessons are that capital punishment is cruel and unusual, that especially in the South it is applied in a racist manner, that humane and defensible alternatives to it are within easy reach, and that Bill Clinton is a calculating opportunist...'.
- 'Governor Bush uses all the surplus for tax cuts, without one new penny for Social Security or the debt. His ad twists the truth like Clinton. We're all pretty tired of that. As president, I'll be conservative and always tell you the truth, no matter what' (Senator John McCain, 2000).

Task 2.9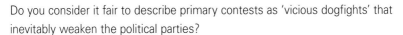

Do you consider it fair to describe primary contests as 'vicious dogfights' that inevitably weaken the political parties?

Guidance

- There have been bitter primary contests such as the Dole–Bush contest in 1988 and the McCain–Bush race in 2000. Candidates are also said to have used crudely opportunistic tactics. Clinton is said to have adopted Republican policies so as to secure the Democratic nomination and the presidency.

Task 2.9 (continued)

- Nonetheless, the primaries do compel those seeking the presidency to campaign and win votes in very different political contexts. There are important cultural contrasts between important primary states. Furthermore, they use different electoral systems (such as caucuses, closed primaries and open primaries). In each of the states, the electorate therefore has a different character. This 'tests' primary candidates to the limit.

How important are the later primaries?

The later stages of the primary season have become increasingly less important. The front-runner usually gains an unassailable lead after the early primaries have taken place. As their fate becomes evident, rivals lose financial backing and campaign staff. They begin to look towards their political futures and are compelled to make their peace with the party's nominee-presumptive. Almost always, only those who are seeking to promote an overtly ideological campaign (such as former California Governor Jerry Brown in 1992, who had campaigned against 'corruption' and 'careerism' in Washington DC) carry their campaigns through to the end of the season and the national convention.

Table 2.9 Democratic primary race, 2004: results

Candidates	Occupation	Home state	Votes	%	Primaries won	Best primary showing (and %)
John Kerry	US senator	Massachusetts	9,961,051	60.7	35	New Jersey (92)
John Edwards	US senator	North Carolina	3,158,205	19.3	1	South Carolina (45)
Howard Dean	Ex-governor	Vermont	936,263	5.7	2	Vermont (54)
Dennis Kucinich	US representative	Ohio	625,148	3.8	—	Oregon (16)
Wesley Clark	Ex-Army general	Arkansas	567,631	3.5	1	Oklahoma (30)

Table 2.9 continued

Candidates	Occupation	Home state	Votes	%	Primaries won	Best primary showing (and %)
Al Sharpton	Minister	New York	396,418	2.4	—	District of Columbia (34)
Joe Lieberman	US senator	Connecticut	282,350	1.7	—	Delaware (11)
Others/ uncommitted			471,036	2.9	—	

Primaries won: Clark (1): Oklahoma. Dean (2): District of Columbia (non-binding), Vermont. Edwards (1): South Carolina. Kerry (35): Alabama, Arizona, Arkansas, California, Connecticut, Delaware, Florida, Georgia, Idaho, Illinois, Indiana, Kentucky, Louisiana, Maryland, Massachusetts, Michigan, Mississippi, Missouri, Montana, Nebraska, New Hampshire, New Jersey, New Mexico, New York, Ohio, Oregon, Pennsylvania, Rhode Island, South Dakota, Tennessee, Texas, Utah, Virginia, West Virginia, Wisconsin.
Note: a non-binding primary is not used as a basis for the election of delegates to a party's national convention.
Source: adapted from www.rhodescook.com/primary.analysis.html

Task 2.10

Why do you think that John Kerry won so many of the 2004 Democratic primaries?

Guidance

You might consider the following points:

- Kerry was seen as a credible presidential candidate because of his long service in the Senate. It was also felt that his Vietnam war record would help deflect charges that the Democrats were not sufficiently patriotic.

- However, there was a more significant reason for Kerry's victories. He won nearly all the later primaries because the contest was decided at a very early stage. Once it was clear that the Kerry campaign had momentum, other candidates found it difficult to attract funding or grassroots volunteers. Only Dennis Kucinich, who put forward a radical platform, continued campaigning, albeit on a shoestring budget.

John Kerry

How fair are criticisms of the primary system?

Although the British political parties have sought to widen the franchise for electing the party leader, in what some observers have seen as an effort to emulate the US system, primaries and caucuses have been subject to sustained criticism. From this perspective, they:

> ...had not produced candidates with mass popular appeal and had proved time-consuming and often prohibitively expensive. The prospect of unwanted nominees foisted by ignorant voters on reluctant party leaders dimmed its luster still further, while to most party officials the primary represented an open invitation to fratricidal conflict.

> Quoted in www.nyu.edu

Task 2.11

How fair is the above quotation about the primary system?

Guidance

- It has already been suggested that leading party figures may play more of a role in determining who takes the nomination than has customarily been recognised. It is certainly difficult to talk of 'unwanted candidates' since Jimmy Carter's successful presidential run in 1976.
- Most party campaigns have pulled together after the tensions and divisions of the primary season. The friction between George W. Bush and John McCain during the race for the 2000 Republican nomination did not prevent Bush winning the presidency (if not the popular vote). Similarly, Bill Clinton won in 1992 despite the earlier splits among Democrats. References to 'fratricidal conflict' therefore seem overstated.

What are the functions of the national conventions?

The presidential and vice-presidential candidates are formally chosen at the national conventions. Held during the summer months, they are attended by delegates from the state parties. Some delegates will be *pledged* (or 'bound') while others are *unpledged*. This means that they are committed, on the basis of their state primary or caucuses, to back the winning candidate (unless released because of that candidate's withdrawal from the race). The overwhelming majority are unpledged. While the Republicans generally use a 'winner-takes-all' system requiring all convention delegates from a state party to support the candidate who won at least a plurality in the primary or caucuses, Democratic primaries and caucuses are proportional. If candidates gain at least 15% of the vote, those seeking the Democratic nomination can win some convention delegates even if they only gained a minority of the votes in a state's primary or caucuses. If a pledged delegate dies or is for some reason unable to attend the convention, an alternative replaces that delegate.

Of the 4,322 total delegates who attended the 2004 Democratic National Convention, 802 were unpledged. Unpledged delegates are generally members of the Democratic National Committee, elected officials such as senators or governors, or leading party figures (the 'superdelegates'). For their part, the Republicans award bonus delegates based upon the party's voting strength in a state. If the Republicans have electoral successes in a state, it gains additional representation. Some critics suggest that this bolsters the hold of the more rural and white state delegations over the convention.

Box 2.3

Convention committees

Three party committees guide the work of the conventions:

(1) The **Credentials Committee** considers the position of delegates, particularly if there are challenges. There was a major credentials battle at the 1964 Democratic Party convention in Atlantic City, New Jersey, when the racially integrated Mississippi Freedom Democratic Party demanded representation in place of the white-only delegation that state party officials had sent. Attempts to reach a compromise failed.

(2) The **Rules Committee** regulates convention procedures. In contrast with the Republicans, the Democrats only adopted a formal rules system in 1972. In some instances, the rules are significant. In 1980, there was a battle over the 'bound delegate' rule which required delegates to vote for the nominee to whom they were pledged at the time of selection.

(3) The **Platform Committee** draws up the platform (setting out principles and policies). Although candidates have often disregarded the platform, it has nonetheless been the subject of controversy. There have been major disputes within the Republican Party about the wording of policy statements on abortion and their place in the platform.

Source: adapted from *Congressional Quarterly* (1997), pp. 85–88

Task 2.12

Examine the table below and answer the question that follows.

Table 2.10 National convention delegates and the voting population, 2004

	Democratic national convention delegates %	Republican national convention delegates %	All voters %
Men	50	57	—
Women	50	43	—
Liberal	41	1	20
Moderate	52	33	42
Conservative	3	63	36
Government should do more to solve national problems	79	7	42
Government is doing too many things	12	85	52
Government should do more to promote traditional values	15	55	40
Government should not favour set of values	78	34	57
USA did the right thing in Iraq	7	96	46
USA should have stayed out of Iraq	86	3	51
Abortion — should be generally available	75	13	34
Abortion should not be permitted	2	38	24
Evangelical/born-again Christian	13	33	34
White	68	85	78
Black	18	6	14
Asian	3	2	2
Hispanic	12	7	11
Firearm in household	33	58	43

Source: adapted *The New York Times*/CBS News (2004)

To what extent did the 2004 national convention delegates 'look like America'?

Guidance

● One would not expect convention delegations to 'look like America'. The delegates are drawn from party activists who, by definition, are strong party identifiers. Attitudes towards abortion and the Iraq war and the proportion of delegates defining themselves as 'conservative' are way out of line with the American electorate as a whole. Nonetheless, the delegates are not entirely unrepresentative.

What have commentators said about the national conventions?

Bifurcated conventions

Byron Shafer has talked about *bifurcated conventions*, and suggests that there are *two* conventions. First, there are decision-making processes. These include deciding on the wording of the party platform and the confirmation of both the presidential candidate and the vice-presidential nominee. Second, there is also a convention that is designed for television and the viewing public. Today's national conventions reflect the shift from 'an older era of brokerage and bargaining to a newer era of publicity and communication' (quoted in Davis 1997, p. 224).

Visible functions of conventions

James W. Davis (1997) suggests that conventions perform six *manifest* (or openly visible) functions:

(1) They nominate candidates and, if the primaries produce no clear winner, they have a 'brokerage' function to overcome the deadlock between the different contenders. (Although the 1952 Republican national convention decided upon Dwight Eisenhower as the candidate, conventions have, since then, merely confirmed the decision made by the primary voters.)

(2) Conventions also encourage party unity. This may be important if there has been a bitter primary contest.

(3) David S. Broder notes that convention delegates may be able to use the national convention to influence the presidential candidate's choice of 'running mate' (p. 232). However, the vice-presidential nominee is now increasingly selected and announced before the national convention takes place. (The 'running mate' may be a defeated rival. In 2004, Senator John Kerry, the Democratic candidate, selected Senator John Edwards.)

(4) Conventions agree the party platform. Issues such as abortion have a history of controversy.

(5) They rally supporters, although in recent years, national campaigning has begun before the convention takes place.

(6) Finally, the convention is '...the supreme governing body of the national party in a predominantly decentralized party system'. It decides on delegate allocations and rules (pp. 231–34).

'Hidden' functions of conventions

National conventions also, however, have *latent* (hidden or implicit) functions. Davis points to the way in which they 'have performed a valuable legitimating function for a nonconsensus candidate' (1997, p. 234). Although Jimmy Carter won only 39% of the votes in the 1976 primary race he was, once nominated, accepted by almost all sections of the Democratic Party as the rightful presidential candidate. Conventions can establish a broad consensus across the 50 state parties as well as the different ideological and sectional groupings that constitute the US national parties. (There have, however, been instances when parties have remained divided. In 1968, against the background of the Vietnam war, the Democratic convention was split between competing factions. This contributed to the victory of Richard Nixon, the Republican candidate in the November contest.)

Task 2.13

Do national conventions serve a significant political purpose?

Guidance

Many observers suggest that national conventions merely confirm the choice of presidential candidate made by voters in the primaries and caucuses. You should explore the reasons why this is often said. However, you could also look, by drawing on specific examples, at instances where the national convention has had rather more significance. In particular, consider the latent functions (see above) of conventions and assess the extent to which they play a role in unifying a party that may have been bitterly divided during the primary season.

Task 2.14

Look closely at Table 2.11 and consider the questions that follow.

Table 2.11 Changes in US presidential nomination process

Before 1968	After 1968
Party 'bosses' largely determined who gained the nomination.	Presidential bids are directed towards the primary voters (although note that party 'elites' play a role in shaping opinion).

Task 2.14 (continued)

Before 1968	After 1968
Some primaries were held to 'test' a candidate's voter appeal.	Most convention delegates are selected through primaries.
Campaigns usually began at the start of the election year.	The 'invisible primary' during the period preceding election year has become increasingly important.
Funding depended upon a relatively small number of wealthy backers. No federal spending limits.	Federal law compels candidates to devote resources to fundraising from large numbers of small contributors and political action committees.
Media coverage was limited.	The media plays an increasingly important role in determining the way in which a candidate is 'framed' and in setting popular expectations for his or her performance. The growth of 24-hour cable news channels has added to the media's importance.
Large states could pick convention delegates at a relatively late stage and still play an important role.	The process has become increasingly 'front-loaded'. The early primaries play a pivotal role.
Conventions could still play a role in determining the party's candidate.	The convention is directed towards the promotion of the candidate to the voting public.

Note: although *Congressional Quarterly (CQ)* suggests that 1968 represented the pivotal turning point, other accounts give different dates or talk in more generalised terms.

Source: adapted from *Congressional Quarterly* (1997), p. 57

(a) In what ways does the table suggest that the presidential nominating process changed after 1968?

(b) To what extent might the table be regarded as an over-simplification?

Guidance
- The table emphasises the opening-up of the nomination process, the declining influence of the party apparatus and the fluid character of the contest.
- Party elites may still play a role in structuring the outcome of the 'invisible primary'. The importance of the earliest primaries is open to question.

Chapter 2

Further reading and references

- Cillizza, C. and Moreno, S. (2006) 'For now, New Hampshire is still first in Democrats' hearts', *The New York Times*, 2 April.
- *Congressional Quarterly* (1997) 'Selecting the President — from 1789 to 1996', pp. 85–88.
- Davis, J. W. (1997) *US Presidential Primaries and the Caucus-Convention System: A Sourcebook*, Greenwood Press.
- Federal Election Commission (2000) *2000 Presidential Primary Election Results*, www.fec.gov
- Fiorina, M. P. with Abrams, S. J. and Pope, J. C. (2005) *Culture War? The Myth of a Polarized America*, Pearson Longman.
- Lamare, J. W., Polinard, J. L. and Wrinkle, R. D. (2003) 'Texas: religion and politics in God's country' in J. C. Green, M. J. Rozell and C. Wilcox (eds) *The Christian Right in American Politics: Marching to the Millennium*, Georgetown University Press, p. 69.
- Norrander, B. (1996) 'Presidential nomination politics in the post-reform era', *Political Research Quarterly*, vol. 49, no. 4, December.
- PBS (1999) 'Quayle bows out', www.pbs.org/newshour
- Rozell, M. J. and Wilcox, C. (2003) 'Virginia: birthplace of the Christian right' in J. C. Green, M. J. Rozell and C. Wilcox (eds) *The Christian Right in American Politics: Marching to the Millennium*, Georgetown University Press, p. 42.
- Toner, R. (2006) 'Democratic group endorses plan for more early primaries', *The New York Times*, 12 March.
- United States Elections Project (2004) 2004 *Presidential Primary Turnout Rates*, http://elections.gmu.edu
- White, J. K. (2003) *The Values Divide: American Politics and Culture in Transition*, Chatham House Publishers.

Does the campaign matter?

What is 'framing'?

Chapter 3 considers the character of the campaign between the different party candidates. (By this time, the Democratic and Republican candidates will have been joined by minor party candidates and independents. For the most part, their candidacies are inconsequential and they may only be on the ballot in a limited number of states.) This chapter examines the tactics employed by Democratic and Republican strategists, the way in which resources are concentrated on particular states, and the structuring of campaigns.

Election strategies are organised around the 'framing' of the candidate. Framing is the construction of the candidate's 'narrative' (or life story). This will have begun during the primary season but will be built upon and consolidated during the post-nomination period. In 2004, Democratic strategists built their representations of Senator John Kerry around his service during the Vietnam war. There were tales about bravery and his devotion to his comrades. Although there were already growing doubts about the wisdom of the Iraq invasion, the Republicans still had a commanding lead among the voting public on national security issues. Significant numbers felt that the USA was safer from both terrorism and external threats if George W. Bush remained in the White House. The challenge for the Democrats was to counter this and shift the public gaze towards other issues and concerns. Kerry therefore appeared before the Democratic national convention and began his address by saluting the delegates. You might take a note of his language:

> I'm John Kerry, and I'm reporting for duty…I defended this country as a young man, and I will defend it as president…I will never hesitate to use force when it is required. Any attack will be met with a swift and certain response…I will never give any nation or international institution a veto over our national security.

At the same time, however, Kerry stressed established Democratic Party themes. He distanced himself from Bush by promising not to privatise Social Security (the system of provision for the elderly); he pointed to rising health care costs and asserted that real wage levels were falling. He also committed himself to a shift in tax policy:

> I will cut middle class taxes. I will reduce the tax burden on small business. And I will roll back the tax cuts for the wealthiest individuals, who make over $200,000 a year, so we can invest in job creation, health care and education.

However, the framing of 'Kerry as war hero' narrative ran into difficulties. First, as Karl Rove (President Bush's principal electoral strategist) remarked, the one item of information that the public had already about Kerry was his service in Vietnam. The convention added nothing new. Second, and more significantly, it opened the way for a Republican-allied group, the Swift Boat Veterans for Truth, to challenge Kerry's account of his own war record. Little could be established with certainty about events in southeast Asia 30 years earlier. The group's claims and the Kerry campaign's counterclaims dominated the news agenda for a significant part of the summer. Whatever the truth, Kerry's credibility was dented and his campaign was unable to shift the agenda onto other issues.

Task 3.1

Describe what is meant by the 'framing' of a candidate. Can you think of any examples other than the Kerry example outlined above?

Guidance

'Framing' refers to the ways in which a candidate's personality and 'narrative' are represented. A candidate's campaign team and his or her opponents will seek to do this in different ways. For example, in 2000, George W. Bush was represented (despite his family ties) as a Washington outsider who brought together resolution, a determination to address law and order issues and a commitment to 'compassionate conservatism'. He was, it was said, pledged to assist the disadvantaged and implement policies drawn from his Christian faith. Of course, Bush's opponents framed him very differently. He came from a privileged background and was a spoiled 'frat boy'. He had little knowledge of government and even less of an understanding of world affairs. There were questions about his competence. At the same time, he was tied to both the interests of oil companies and extremist forms of religion.

Why are some states more important than others?

'Swing' states

In first-past-the-post systems, candidates almost always concentrate their resources on certain seats. In both Britain and the USA, some simply cannot be won. In others, a candidate may be assured of victory. Republicans, for example, face formidable obstacles in Congressional Districts where there is a majority of African-Americans. They are the most loyal of the groupings that lean towards the Democrats and a Democratic candidate is more or less certain to secure election. Energy and resources are therefore devoted to marginal seats. These are dubbed 'swing' or sometimes 'battleground' states.

In 1960, Richard Nixon, the Republican candidate, committed himself to visiting all 50 states during the course of his campaign. During the last weekend before election day, he flew to Alaska to fulfil his promise. In contrast, John F. Kennedy, his Democratic rival, campaigned in the 'swing states' of the northeast and won. The Nixon campaign lost ground. Eight years later, in 1968, when Nixon stood again, he was careful not to repeat the mistake.

As the 2004 contest approached, the result in some states seemed assured. The Kerry campaign was particularly confident of victory in states on the east and west coasts. Although both had Republican governors, New York and California were seen as safely Democratic. For their part, the Republicans were confident of Texas and a swathe of largely rural midwestern, mountain and southern states.

However, some states were bitterly contested. Neither party was sure of success. In 2000, the result in Florida had been the subject of a bitter fight and there was a struggle again in 2004. Other battleground states included Ohio and Missouri.

Task 3.2

Why are 'swing' states so important in election campaigns?

Guidance

Although some forms of electioneering have a national character, intense campaigning tends to be confined to the 'swing' states. In a close contest, however, even small swing states with very few Electoral College Votes (see Chapter 4) will form part of the battleground.

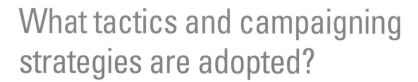

What tactics and campaigning strategies are adopted?

Adopting the 'middle ground'

The battle to win the swing states determines the tactics that are adopted. In both 1992 and 1996, Bill Clinton sought to reach out beyond traditional Democratic voters by adopting themes more usually associated with the Republican Party. He backed the death penalty, called for 'small government' and spoke of the need for welfare reform to end dependency. He styled himself, in a slogan that was to be adopted across the Atlantic, a 'new Democrat'. In 2000, George W. Bush associated himself with 'compassionate conservatism'. He distanced himself from both Congressional Republicans and the Christian right who were seen as unduly abrasive by significant groups of voters. Like Clinton, he hoped to win over the middle ground or moderate vote.

Distance from the party

In the past, candidates have pursued the moderate and unaligned vote by eschewing partisan labels. In the 1950s, Dwight Eisenhower distanced himself from the Republican Party, which had nominated him. In 1972, the Committee to Re-Elect the President, which is remembered because of its role in the Watergate scandal, was an attempt to move beyond party labels.

Adopting ideological positions

Barry Goldwater

Other campaigns have been rooted in party and ideology. However, they have generally been unsuccessful. In 1964, Senator Barry Goldwater, the Republican candidate, adopted an uncompromisingly conservative platform. As he put it: 'extremism in the defense of liberty is no vice. And moderation in the pursuit of justice is no virtue'. It was relatively easy, given this, for the Democrats to portray Goldwater as an extremist. Although only shown once, an early television 'attack ad' played upon fears of nuclear war and, by implication, suggested that Goldwater might prove reckless. Goldwater secured just 52 Electoral College Votes. (The Electoral College is the mechanism by which US presidents are elected. It is an indirect system based upon states rather than individual votes. To win a state and secure election, candidates must gain a simple majority within a state.) In a landslide victory (although one magnified by the first-past-the-post system used by the College), President Lyndon Johnson was returned with 486.

In 1972, against a background of the Vietnam war and the emerging counter-culture, the Democrats selected Senator George McGovern as their presidential candidate. He campaigned against the war and committed himself to redis-tributive government programmes. He gained just 17 Electoral College Votes. Richard Nixon secured 520.

'Energising the base'

It has been suggested that the dynamics of electoral campaigns have changed since the 1980s. As the 2004 election approached, there seemed to be relatively few undecided, unaligned or middle-ground votes. Instead, there was evidence of long-term polarisation. Those formerly in the middle had, it was said, taken sides and those voters already committed to the Democratic or Republican camps had hardened their opinions. Supporters of President Bush seemed to despise John Kerry. Democratic supporters appeared to hate the president. The media contributed to the charged atmosphere. Fox News, which barely sought to hide its backing for the Republicans, ridiculed Democrats. Films by radical directors such as Michael Moore attacked Bush in vitriolic terms. Against this background, commentators suggested that the 2004 campaign strategies were therefore directed towards increasing turnout by the parties' 'natural' backers rather than winning the loyalty of the small numbers left in the middle ground. This required uncompromising appeals rather than moderation. The task was to 'energise the base'.

There is evidence to support this picture. In a number of states, Republicans emphasised controversial moral issues such as same-sex marriage. This may well have encouraged churchgoers who might have otherwise stayed at home to cast a vote. However, there were also efforts to win over the middle ground. Relatively moderate 'security moms' (married women with children who were concerned about the threat posed by terrorism and international instability) were also courted with a considerable degree of success.

Task 3.3

In what ways have recent election campaigns appealed to the party's 'base' and middle-ground voters?

Guidance

Recent campaigns have sought to 'energise the base' and win over 'undecideds'. In 2000, Al Gore (the Democrats' presidential candidate) attacked the pharmaceutical companies and other corporate interests. He used language that won plaudits from the Democratic Party faithful, many of whom have long been critical of big business. At the same time, however, his campaign sought to reassure moderate voters, particularly those who had been disturbed or alienated by President Bill Clinton's affair with Monica Lewinsky and his subsequent impeachment. Gore stressed the strength of his own family relationships and nominated Senator Joseph Lieberman as his vice-presidential running mate. Lieberman had been particularly critical of Clinton's behaviour and had always stressed both his religious faith (Judaism) and his backing for the principles associated with moral traditionalism.

What role does the vice-presidential nominee play?

Vice-presidential campaigns were traditionally selected to 'balance the ticket'. To win the broadest electoral support for a campaign, the running mate would be drawn from a very different background. He or she would come from a contrasting region and represent a different wing of the party. In recent years, however, there has been a narrowing of the criteria for selecting the vice-presidential nominee. He or she is now chosen to correct a perceived fault or weakness in the presidential candidate. In 1992, Bill Clinton was seen (as governor of Arkansas) as a Washington outsider and tainted by scandal. Al Gore did not balance the Democratic ticket in the traditional sense. He was, like Clinton, a southerner, a member of a Southern Baptist church and associated with the modernising wing of the party. However, he was a senator and had a seemingly unblemished personal life. In 2000, George W. Bush had been widely portrayed as inexperienced and ignorant of international politics. He therefore selected Dick Cheney, an experienced 'heavyweight' Washington insider, as his running mate. Arguably, Cheney's experience and relative gravitas allowed him to become the most powerful vice-president in US history.

The running mate always takes second place in an election campaign. Indeed, he or she may remain almost unobserved for long periods. At times, there have been hopes that he or she will play more of a role. In 2004, it was expected that John Kerry's choice of John Edwards, another senator who had challenged Kerry in the primaries, would add dynamism and *élan* to the Democrats' presidential bid. Edwards was a relatively young and vigorous campaigner. However, he had a low profile during almost all of the campaign. Other vice-presidential choices have led to embarrassment. Dan Quayle, George H. W. Bush's vice-presidential pick in 1988, caused difficulties when questions were asked about his military service and his failure to serve in Vietnam. There were also questions about the only woman to be represented on a major party's presidential ticket. Geraldine Ferraro's tax returns (and those of her husband) came under close scrutiny during the 1984 campaign when she was picked as the Democrats' vice-presidential nominee.

Dick Cheney and John Edwards on the televised 2004 vice-presidential debate

The now established televised debate between the vice-presidential nominees (which takes place in between presidential debates) allows the running mate to establish more of a profile. Liz Marlantes reported on the 2004 vice-presidential debate between Dick Cheney and John Edwards for *The Christian Science Monitor*:

> ...A definite contrast in styles — Cheney came across as serious, sober, even-keeled. To some extent, I thought he was even less animated than usual...Edwards came across as sincere, empathetic. The trial lawyer in him was evident — he repeatedly picked up on things Cheney said, and appealed to viewers as though they were a jury, using emotional and sometimes personal anecdotes to make his case...both candidates were strongly on the attack. Cheney spent a great deal of time ripping into Kerry's record — both calling him a flip-flopper and also portraying him as an anti-defense and pro-tax liberal who wants to expand the reach of government. He also portrayed Edwards as inexperienced and shallow...Edwards hit back on the administration's record on jobs and Iraq...

It probably won't have a huge impact either way — vice presidential debates typically don't unless someone makes a huge gaffe, which didn't happen tonight. For partisans on both sides, it probably reinforced impressions that they already held — Cheney likely came across to staunch Republicans as experienced and tough; while to staunch Democrats he likely seemed dour and out of touch; Edwards likely struck Democrats as compassionate and sharp, but Republicans probably saw him as shallow and glib…

Task 3.4

What does the running mate bring to a presidential campaign?

Guidance

The running mate has sometimes been a drag on the campaign because of revelations that have been made after his or her selection. There are few examples of vice-presidential nominees adding all that much to a campaign, although their role in 'correcting' an apparent 'fault' or weakness in the presidential candidate should not be underestimated. His or her role in the televised debates is largely confined to the avoidance of error and much depends upon the established perceptions of the viewer and listener.

What is the 'permanent campaign'?

An election campaign is usually associated with the months preceding the November contest and, to a lesser extent and in a more hidden form, the 'invisible primary'. However, since the beginning of the 1980s, commentators have discussed the 'permanent campaign'. This is, according to Hugh Heclo, 'a nonstop process seeking to manipulate sources of public approval to engage in the act of governing itself' (quoted in American Enterprise Institute (2000), Summary). In other words, the dividing line between campaigning and governing has been largely erased. Furthermore, of the two, campaigning has become progressively more important. For Charles Jones and other commentators, the Clinton administration in particular seemed to be structured around a continuous campaign. His years in the White House were structured around re-election and efforts to secure a Democratic victory in the 2000 presidential election:

The permanent campaign means that campaigns are nonstop and year-round and that the process of governing and campaigning takes place in a continuous loop. Campaign consultants move without pause from the campaign trail to work for the victorious elected officials and help to shape their policy messages and frame issues for advantage in the next campaign…When policy and political aides leave White House, Senate, or House staffs, they regularly join campaign consulting shops or lobbying operations…Legislative proposals, routinely subjected to intense polling and focus groups before they are launched, are thereafter monitored by tracking polls…As elections approach, many of those groups run 'issue' advertising campaigns, indistinguishable from electioneering, that target candidates directly, often with less issue content than any other kind of advertising, including that of the candidates…The permanent campaign takes place on the campaign trail, on the airwaves, on the floors of the House and Senate, in the Oval Office, and increasingly in the courts and in law offices.

Ornstein and Mann (2000)

However, the celebrated political commentator Joe Klein (2005) has suggested that George W. Bush's administration may have taken the permanent campaign a stage further:

George W. Bush may be the very best. Indeed, his Administration represents the final, squalid perfection of the Permanent Campaign: a White House where almost every move is tactical, a matter of momentary politics, even decisions that involve life and death and war…Bush's White House is a conundrum, a bastion of telegenic idealism and deep cynicism. The President has proposed vast, transformational policies — the remaking of the Middle East, of Social Security, of the federal bureaucracy. But he has done so in a haphazard way, with little attention to detail or consequences. There are grand pronouncements and, yes, crusades, punctuated with marching words like evil and moral and freedom. Beneath, though, is the cynical assumption that the public doesn't care about the details — that results don't matter, corners can be cut and special favors bestowed.

Writing in the *Arizona Daily Star* (30 March 2004), Kathryn Dunn Tenpas and Anthony Corrado have pointed to the Bush administration's awareness of electoral considerations and the need to 'nurture' the 'swing states':

…Bush out-traveled President Clinton (302 domestic trips) who, by many accounts, was thought to be the most political of presidents…Bush has spent the bulk of his time in swing general election states — the 16 states that were each decided in 2000 by the narrowest of margins — 6 percent of the vote or less. In his first year, 36 percent of Bush's domestic travel consisted of visits to swing states; in year two, 45 percent; in year three, 39 percent. By comparison, Clinton focused his travel in swing states 28 percent of the time in year one, 33 percent in year two and 39 percent in the third year…In short, Bush has out-traveled and out-targeted Clinton.

As Ornstein and Mann suggest, the permanent campaign shapes Congressional life as well as White House decision making. Politics are subordinated to the needs of the electoral cycle. There were, for example, frequent suggestions that Senator Bill Frist, who was leading the Republicans in the Senate, was determining legislative priorities on the basis of coming elections and with his own potential 2008 presidential bid in mind. His decision not to find space in the legislative timetable for votes on measures to impose on networks and presenters who broadcast allegedly indecent material was said to reflect Frist's efforts to court moderate votes

by distancing himself from the Christian right. However, other issues, most notably tax concerns, were accorded time on the Senate floor. As Sheryl Gay Stolberg wrote in *The New York Times* on 15 February 2006, 10 months ahead of the mid-term elections:

> The Senate has never been a bastion of managerial efficiency. But…lawmakers say things are clearly getting worse.
>
> Four cabinet secretaries, including Secretary of State Condoleezza Rice, an Army general and the secretary of the Army were supposed to testify Tuesday morning at hearings on matters including Hurricane Katrina and the Bush administration's budget for foreign affairs.
>
> But their invitations were rescinded and the hearings canceled when the Senate majority leader, Bill Frist of Tennessee, scheduled a marathon series of 16 votes on amendments to a pending tax bill — all of them, both parties agree, intended more to score political points than to make policy.

Task 3.5

To what extent do you consider the US policy-making process to be governed by the 'permanent campaign'?

Guidance

Many writers stress the extent to which daily life and political considerations in both the White House and on Capitol Hill are subordinated to electoral needs. Joe Klein applies this in a graphic way to the Bush administration, arguing that domestic policy and the absence of detailed planning for the Iraq war were shaped by a concern to secure votes. However, it could be useful to consider the extent to which this is a recent development. Some might be tempted to argue that 'twas ever thus'.

Task 3.6

Read this extract from the influential Washington-based periodical *Congressional Quarterly (CQ)* and answer the question that follows.

What is the role of the media?

> The mass media…are playing an increasingly important role in presidential elections largely because they serve as the dominant source of information about candidates and elections for most Americans — more than family, friends, associates, and direct contacts with political parties and candidate organizations. The media also have taken over many of the 'intermediary' functions of party organizations, linking voters with the larger political system. News sources appear to be the most influential early in the

Task 3.6 (continued)

nominating process when 'horse-race' coverage of the primaries helps to winnow the candidates. At that time, the media help the public to form impressions of the large field of candidates, many of whom may be unfamiliar. By the time of the general election, voters are more likely to have set feelings about the candidates — making it more difficult for media coverage to influence them.

Congressional Quarterly (CQ) (1997), pp. 106–07

To what extent, according to *Congressional Quarterly (CQ)*, do the media influence the electoral process?

Guidance

CQ draws an important distinction between the different stages of the electoral process. The extract also includes some comments that have implications for the debate about the 'decline' of the major political parties.

Further reading and references

- American Enterprise Institute (2000) *The Permanent Campaign and its Future*, Washington DC, www.aei.org/books/bookID.188.filter.all/book_detail2.asp
- CNN (2004) '"Help is on the way," Kerry tells middle class: Democrat accepts nomination, courts the undecideds', 30 July, www.cnn.com
- Dunn Tenpas, K. and Corrado, A. (2004) 'Permanent campaign brushes aside tradition', *Arizona Daily Star*, 30 March.
- Klein, J. (2005) 'The perils of the permanent campaign: Can the public live with an administration that is cutting corners and ignoring the details?' *Time*, 30 October.
- Marlantes, L. (2004) 'Q&A: Vice presidential debate', *The Christian Science Monitor*, 7 October, www.csmonitor.com
- Ornstein, N. J. and Mann, T. E. (eds) (2000) *The Permanent Campaign and its Future*, The AEI Press, www.aei.org/books/bookID.188,filter.all/book_detail2.asp
- Stolberg, S. G. (2006) 'Senate scrubs hearings as politics trump policy in an election year', *The New York Times*, 15 February.

Is the Electoral College defensible?

Chapter 4 surveys the process that occurs after the people have cast their votes. It will look at the Electoral College and the 'Electors', the requirements imposed by the US Constitution, and the ways in which the College can, in some circumstances, affect the final election outcome.

What is the Electoral College?

The USA has an indirect system for choosing its presidents based upon the Electoral College. Members of the College are called 'Electors'. Once the popular election has been held and the number of votes confirmed, Electors meet in their respective state capitals and cast 'Electoral Votes'. The number is based upon a state's Congressional representation, which is, in turn, dependent upon the relative population size of each state. There are 538 Electoral College Votes in total. A simple majority (270) is required for a candidate to secure the presidency.

Who are the Electors?

Electors are often selected in recognition of their service for their political party. They may be state-elected officials, party leaders, or people who have a personal or political affiliation with the presidential candidate. Voters in each state then choose the Electors on the day of the general election. The Electors' names may or may not appear on the ballot below the name of the candidates running for president, depending on the procedure in each state. The parties put forward their own slates of Electors who serve if a party's candidate wins a plurality of the popular vote in the state. However, in 42 states and the District of Columbia, the presidential 'short ballot' is used. It makes the election process much more straightforward. The voters can immediately see who they are casting a ballot for. The ordinary voter does not see the names of these Electors. Instead, the ballot only shows the names of the presidential and vice-presidential candidates. The voters are nonetheless choosing Electors who are charged with formally determining who should serve as president.

Although proposed by the principal parties, the process for selecting Electors differs between states. In 26, they are chosen by state party conventions. Eight states and the District of Columbia (Washington DC) require nomination by state or district party committees, and 14 allow the parties to choose their own method of selection (Fortier 2004, p. 6).

> Box 4.1
> **Timeline for the 2008 presidential election — voting and after**
>
> **4 November** Election day
>
> **4 November–9 December** Period for resolving state recounts, challenges and controversies
>
> **15 December (first Monday after the second Wednesday in December)** Electors cast their votes
>
> **6 January** Congress counts the Electoral Votes
>
> **20 January** Inauguration day
>
> Source: adapted from Fortier (2004), p. xv

Why was the Electoral College established?

It is often said that the College was created because the Framers, or 'Founding Fathers' who wrote the US Constitution, distrusted the people. This is part of the explanation. However, John C. Fortier (2004, pp. 66–67) suggests that their deliberations were guided by three principal considerations:

(1) The College was a compromise between those who sought to maintain the decentralised system of government offered by the Articles of Confederation that preceded the creation of the USA. It was a way of heading off the calls of those who wished the president to be chosen by the state legislatures (thereby bolstering states' rights) of election and transferring a degree of power to the people (or at least those among those who were enfranchised).

(2) There were fears that a national popular election was not feasible in a large country where distances seemed vast and communication was slow. Furthermore, if national elections were held, the electorate would inevitably have little knowledge of the candidates. People would be unable to make an informed or 'national' decision. They might simply vote on the basis of localism for a candidate from their own state. In the Federalist Papers that were written to canvass support for the US Constitution, Alexander Hamilton noted: 'A small

Alexander Hamilton

number of persons, selected by their fellow citizens from the general mass, will be most likely to possess the information and discernment requisite to such complicated investigations.'

(3) Each state had different laws and traditions governing those who were eligible to vote. It would be difficult, probably impossible, to reconcile these and regulate the franchise on a national basis.

Task 4.1

To what extent are the Framers' reasons for creating the Electoral College still valid today?

Guidance

Many of the arguments are now outdated. The creation of a national franchise (through successive Constitutional amendments) means that, for the most part, states no longer determine who can, and who cannot, vote. (However, many states still limit the voting rights of those who have served a prison sentence.) Nonetheless, the College is one of the few institutionalised mechanisms in the Constitution that provide a role for the states. Many supporters of the present system talk in terms of 'states' rights' as well as pointing to the disadvantages associated with alternative systems and structures.

What are 'faithless Electors'?

The term 'faithless Electors' is applied to those who consciously or unconsciously fail to cast their vote for the candidate who won the popular vote in their state. About half the states have legislation requiring Electors to follow the wishes of the electorate and vote for the candidate who gained the most popular votes (although in many cases no penalty is specified and there is no record of a prosecution). Electors in the other states, however, are not legally bound to vote for a specific candidate (see Table 4.1). However, federal law does allow Congress to reject Electoral Votes when the two chambers 'agree that such vote or votes have not been so regularly given by electors' (National Archives and Records Administration, 2005).

There have been nine 'faithless Electors' in US history. There were instances in both 2000 and 2004. In 2000, a Democratic Elector in Washington DC cast a blank ballot instead of voting for Al Gore. This was, she said, a protest against the lack of representation in Congress for the District of Columbia (because it is not a state). In a comment on her action, she referred to DC's 'colonial status'. In 2004, a Democratic Elector in Minnesota wrote 'John Ewards' on his or her

Table 4.1 States that do *not* legally bind their Electors to vote for the popular vote winner

State	Number of Electoral Votes
Arizona	10
Arkansas	6
Delaware	3
Georgia	15
Idaho	4
Illinois	21
Indiana	11
Iowa	7
Kansas	6
Kentucky	8
Louisiana	9
Minnesota	10
Missouri	11
New Hampshire	4
New Jersey	15
New York	31
North Dakota	3
Pennsylvania	21
Rhode Island	4
South Dakota	3
Tennessee	11
Texas	34
Utah	5
West Virginia	5

Source: National Archives and Records Administration (2005)

ballot. This was deemed to be a vote for Senator John Edwards, who had been the Democratic running mate. The process was a secret ballot and it is not known whether the vote was deliberate or accidental.

What conclusions should be drawn about the Electoral College after the 2000 presidential election?

Those opposed to the Electoral College point to 'faithless Electors', who defy the popular will by voting for a candidate other than the winner of the popular vote in their state. They also emphasise the way in which the College 'discriminates'

against minor party candidates (unless their votes are concentrated in particular states) and over-represents the least populous states.

For the most part, however, critics cite the outcome of the 2000 election. After a prolonged dispute about the counting process and the validity of some votes in Florida, George W. Bush secured a narrow majority in the Electoral College and thereby secured the presidency. Nonetheless, Al Gore, the Democratic candidate, had won a majority of the popular vote across the country.

This, it was said, highlighted the fundamentally undemocratic character of the College. It uses a winner-takes-all or first-past-the-post system in almost every state, whereby the candidate with more votes than the runner-up (which may be a simple plurality rather than a majority, i.e. at least one more vote than the runner-up) gains all of that state's Electoral College votes. A huge popular majority has the same weight as the narrowest of victories. In certain circumstances, the winner of the popular vote can therefore lose in the Electoral College.

However, there are only two circumstances in which such a scenario is likely. It may arise if an election is close. It could also happen where there are more than two credible candidates in the general election. The election in 2000 was a closely fought contest between Al Gore (Democrat) and George W. Bush (Republican). Although the minor party candidates, most notably Ralph Nader (Green) and Patrick J. Buchanan (a hardline conservative and former Republican who turned to the Reform Party) had no chance of victory, they were able to play a significant role because in such a close contest every vote mattered.

> The 2000 election was an extraordinary event, unlikely to be seen again in any of our lifetimes. It had been over one hundred years since the winner of the popular vote did not also win a majority in the electoral college…it is true that we are in a period of parity between the parties, with the presidency, Congress, and control of state governments up for grabs for Democrats and Republicans. However, even this close competition is unlikely to result in a dead heat in a single state, whose outcome would determine the winner of a majority of the electoral college.
>
> Fortier (2004), pp. 46–47

Task 4.2

(a) Why does Fortier suggest that it is rare for one candidate to win the popular vote while another secures a majority in the Electoral College?

(b) Do you think that this is a credible argument for retaining the Electoral College?

Task 4.2 (continued)

Guidance

Consider these points when answering the questions:

- Fortier argues that the 2000 result was a consequence of the candidates being so evenly matched, in terms of votes, across the country. It would not have happened, he asserts, if there had been a larger gap between them.
- However, the election does not have to be very close for the winner of the popular vote to lose the Electoral Vote and vice versa. In the 2004 contest, Bush won the popular vote with 52% of the popular two-party vote. Indeed, he was the first candidate since his father (in 1988) to win a majority of the popular vote. However, if 60,000 votes that were cast for George W. Bush had instead been given to John Kerry, Kerry would have secured Ohio's 20 Electoral College Votes thereby giving him the presidency.

Box 4.2

What are the electoral consequences of reapportionment?

In the long term, the US centre of population is shifting in a southwesterly direction. In other words, in relative terms, states in the south and west are gaining population at a faster rate than those in other regions, particularly the northeast.

A process of reapportionment follows the census. This means that Congressional representation, and therefore Electoral College Votes, are reassigned on the basis of population shifts. Therefore, in 2004, if George W. Bush had won exactly the same states as he won in 2000, he would have won the Electoral College Vote by a margin of 278–260, a net gain of 7 Electoral Votes over the 2000 result. Many of the southern and western states leaned towards the Republicans. While the increase in population can in part be attributed to Latino population growth, and Latinos lean disproportionately towards the Democrats, many are not citizens or are not registered to vote.

Task 4.3

Read the extract from Walter Berns and answer the questions that follow.

> ...to see the case for the present system of electing the president requires a shift in point of view from that usually taken by the critics [of the Electoral College]. They tend to view elections in terms of *input* — in terms of the right to vote, equal weight of votes, who in fact votes, and the like. The framers [of the Constitution] thought it at least as important to consider the *output* of any

Task 4.3 (continued)

given electoral system. What kind of men does it bring to office? How will it affect the working of the political system? What is its bearing on the political character of the whole country?

Berns (2004), pp. 53–54

(a) What does Berns mean by 'inputs' and 'outputs'?

(b) Do you agree with his evaluation of the College and the electoral process?

Guidance

- Berns is referring, when he talks of 'inputs', to the voting process and the actions of the electorate. By 'outputs', he means the result of elections.
- Berns' questions tend to suggest that because the Electoral College has produced presidents of stature, and a political system that is widely admired, it has legitimacy. Nonetheless, others might contend, the large numbers who do not vote (perhaps, in part, because campaigning is not directed towards 'safe' states) suggest that all is not well.

Box 4.3

What happens if no candidate gains a majority in the Electoral College?

If no candidate gains a majority of the Electoral Votes, the election is decided by the (newly elected) House of Representatives. Under the terms of the 12th Amendment, the House chooses between the three candidates with the greatest number of Electoral Votes. However, in voting, each state has only one vote.

> The Framers of the Constitution originally thought that most presidential elections would be deadlocked. George Mason, for one, predicted that nineteen out of twenty elections would be decided by the House. In fact, only two presidential elections — those of 1800 and 1824, have been so decided.
>
> *Congressional Quarterly* (1997), p. 125

For its part, the Senate chooses the vice-president. If no candidate gains a majority, then there is a run-off contest between the two candidates with the most votes.

Task 4.4

Why might these provisions be considered unfair?

Guidance

The system might be said to breach the separation of powers. Furthermore, if every state has only one vote, this offers a significant advantage to the least populous states. These tend to be relatively conservative and traditionalist in character.

Box 4.4

What happens if there is no president or vice-president?

Under the 1947 Presidential Succession Act of 1947 (but not the Constitution), there is a line of succession that is to be followed if '...by reason of death, resignation, removal from office, inability, or failure to qualify...' there is no president or vice-president.

The 'powers and duties' of the presidency then pass to the Speaker of the House of Representatives, the President *pro tempore* of the Senate (generally the longest-serving member of the majority party), and then the members of cabinet in the order that their departments were established. The list begins with the Secretary of State and ends with the Secretary of Veterans' Affairs. At the time of writing, the Secretary of Homeland Security, the most recently created department, had yet to be added.

In *The West Wing* (Series 5), the vice-president has resigned. Shortly afterwards, President Bartlet's daughter is kidnapped. He steps down from the presidency on a temporary basis (citing the 25th Amendment of the Constitution). In such circumstances, the powers of the presidency have to pass to the Speaker of the House. In contrast with Bartlet, the Speaker is a committed conservative.

Task 4.5

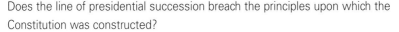

Does the line of presidential succession breach the principles upon which the Constitution was constructed?

Guidance

It might be argued that because the line of succession passes, after the vice-president, to the Speaker of the House and then the President *pro tempore* of the Senate before passing to cabinet officers, that the separation of powers has been breached.

Further reading and references

- Berns, W. (2004) 'Let's hear it for the Electoral College', in J. C. Fortier (ed.) *After the People Vote: A Guide to the Electoral College*, pp. 53–54.
- *Congressional Quarterly* (1997) 'Selecting the President – from 1789 to 1996', p. 125.
- Fortier, J. C. (ed.) (2004) *After the People Vote: A Guide to the Electoral College*, The AEI Press.
- National Archives and Records Administration (2005) *Presidential Election Laws — United States Code*, www.archives.gov/federal-register
- National Archives and Records Administration (2005) *What is the Electoral College?* www.archives.gov/federal-register

What factors determine Congressional elections?

There are some similarities between presidential and Congressional elections. Although there are partisan loyalties among voters, parties play only a limited role in the organisation of campaigns and in shaping the political careers of the candidates. Instead, both presidential and Congressional elections are candidate-centred. However, there are also important differences. In Congressional elections, the incumbent has important advantages if he or she is standing. Although there are national 'mood swings', local issues can be pivotal in a particular state or district. Chapter 5 considers all these issues.

Are elections candidate-centred?

Many observers think so. Most recent observers have stressed the candidate-centred character of Congressional elections, particularly in the House of Representatives. From this perspective, the focus for voters is on the candidates and they, rather than the parties, direct the election campaigns. As Morris Fiorina has noted:

> Members of Congress were particularly adept at developing electoral techniques that enabled them to personalize their electoral coalitions. Increasingly, they were able to avoid association with their party's larger issues of national policy. Instead, they were able to win on the basis of their personal characteristics, their personal policy positions, their record of service to the district, and the great resource advantages that enabled them to discourage strong challengers and beat those whom they could not discourage.
>
> Quoted in Stonecash et al. (2003), pp. 132–33

David R. Mayhew has spoken in broadly similar terms:

> No theoretical treatment of the United States Congress that posits parties as analytic units will go very far…The best service a party can supply to its congressmen is a

negative one; it can leave them alone. And this in general is what the congressional parties do.

Quoted in Stonecash et al. (2003), p. 133

Why have parties appeared to have lost their former importance? There are four interrelated reasons:

(1) Mayhew has stressed the role of primaries. Election and re-election depend upon a candidate's own efforts (rather than the party apparatus) and his or her ability to reflect the hopes and aspirations of grassroots supporters.

> The establishment of primaries during the early 1900s started the reduction of a party role in influencing nominations...This freedom has prompted House candidates to organize their own campaigns, raise their own resources, and, if they are incumbents, exploit the resources that accompany being a member of the House to gain reelection.
>
> Quoted in Stonecash et al. (2003), p. 132

(2) Dealignment, a decline in the proportion of committed party identifiers, may also have played a role by creating a context within which candidates could assert their autonomy. From the 1950s, established party loyalties began to weaken. In particular, the proportion of strong party identifiers fell. There was more 'split-ticket voting'. (However, dealignment was not a continuing or consistent process. Republican identification increased as the party won the backing of white southerners and evangelical church-goers. There may also have been an increase in the proportion of strong party identifiers during the Clinton and Bush years as political battles assumed a more bitter and partisan form.)

(3) The parties were traditionally dominated by 'bosses' who secured loyalty through the 'spoils system', with, for example, the promise of municipal employment. Contemporary ethics have curtailed the 'spoils system'. The era of the 'boss' who often had the party within his grip and upon whom prospective candidates were dependent is now over.

(4) The states and regions of the USA have different interests and cultures. In particular, there is a divide between many of the metropolitan areas and the more rural 'heartland' states. The metropolitan areas have a multi-racial and multi-ethnic character and also include significant liberal enclaves. The 'heartland' states are largely white and are much more rural. They tend to be more conservative and traditionalist. As Ross English notes:

> A Democrat seeking election from a constituency covering New York City would find it difficult to succeed if she adopted the same policy positions and priorities as a fellow Democrat in, say, rural Kansas. It would be folly for any party to expect candidates to do otherwise.
>
> English (2003), p. 19

However, the extent to which the Congressional electoral process has become candidate-centred is open to argument. First, the parties play an important part in fundraising through Congressional 'leadership' committees. Second, despite the growth of primaries, senior party figures (sometimes described as the 'party establishment') are, in practice, able to influence the outcome of primary races. For example, Paul Hackett, an Iraqi war veteran who opposed US intervention, complained that prominent Democratic Party senators had deterred him from standing in an Ohio Senate race by calling his donors and urging them to withdraw their backing. They did this, it was said, to ensure that a stronger candidate would do battle against the Republican incumbent (Urbina, 2006).

The Ohio Senate race was not an isolated instance. As *The Washington Post* reported in February 2006, influential Democrats were also seeking to influence the primary race in an open Illinois House contest (see Box 5.1).

Box 5.1
How are candidates recruited?

Reaching to shake hands with a voter, she says: 'You may have heard of me. I'm the Iraq war vet who's running. I was injured over there.' Talking with another, she says: 'I actually lost both my legs. I can walk because I got really good health care.'

Tammy Duckworth, Democratic candidate for Congress, cannot escape the catastrophic wounds she suffered as an Army helicopter pilot in Iraq. And, for the purposes of her candidacy, she does not want to. For better or worse, her injuries are her signature, her motivator and, she hopes, her ticket into the consciousness of voters in the Illinois 6th District.

'I can't avoid the interest in the fact that I'm an injured female soldier,' Duckworth, 37, says in an interview at her campaign headquarters in Lombard, west of Chicago. 'Understand that I'm going to use this as a platform.'

That is just what a pair of influential Illinois Democrats expected when they recruited her to seek the seat surrendered after 32 years by Republican stalwart Henry J. Hyde. Sen. Richard J. Durbin and Rep. Rahm Emanuel appealed to Duckworth when she was still recovering from her injuries, dissing the up-and-running campaign of fellow Democrat Christine Cegelis, who took 44 percent of the vote against Hyde in 2004.

Duckworth, who considers the Iraq war a mistake, is among about a dozen veterans who served in Iraq or Afghanistan running for federal office this year, at last count all but one of them Democrats. The party leadership is calculating that candidates who wore the uniform can offer a credible counterpoint on national security to Republicans who have dominated the debate from the campaign trail to Capitol Hill.

Slevin (2006)

There are, however, some constraints. In some cases, those seeking nomination may defy the party 'establishment'. In Florida, Katherine Harris (who was Secretary of State of the 'Sunshine State' at the time of the 2000 election and, as such, had been closely associated with attempts to end the recounting process and award the state's Electoral College Votes to George W. Bush and thereby give him the presidency) was seeking the Republican Party's nomination as a 2006 senatorial candidate. According to *The New Republic*, leading party figures in Washington (and Robert Dole, the Republicans' 1996 presidential nominee) feared that she would lose the general election because, through her associations with the disputed 2000 election, she was too divisive a figure. They therefore sought out alternative candidates but no one of stature would join the race (see Box 5.2).

Box 5.2

Party crasher

Soon after Harris declared her candidacy, Dole and others publicly courted Florida House Speaker Allan Bense, Representative Mark Foley, former Army General Tommy Franks, and even the representative-turned-TV-host Joe Scarborough, but to no avail. Beyond the national dynamics that make such Republicans wary of risking their necks this fall was another daunting factor: Harris's beloved status among GOP partisans. 'Katherine Harris is strong as battery acid in a primary,' says Republican pollster Whit Ayres, 'and enormously polarizing in the general.' By January, Republicans finally seemed resigned to Harris's candidacy. At a January 21 meeting of Republican activists, Jeb Bush said he would give her his 'strong support,' a public signal that the Stop Harris movement has ended. And, when he visited Florida last weekend, George Bush invited Harris to ride with him on Air Force One.

Crowley (2006)

President Bush and candidate-centred elections

President George W. Bush used the White House to define national campaign themes, assist with fundraising and boost particular candidates. In the 2002 mid-term elections, Bush's popularity (in the wake of the September 11th attacks) was regarded as a major asset for the Republicans. Indeed, although it is usually only applied to presidential elections, it is legitimate to talk of a 'coat-tails effect'.

George W. Bush

In 2006, President Bush's approval ratings had slumped. Nonetheless, Bush still played a significant role. Eight months ahead of the election, he attacked the Democrats, arguing that they were dangerously weak and indecisive on national security and would damage the economy by raising taxes. He held a buffet lunch, asking for $1,000 from those who wished to attend and $10,000 for photographs with him. He threw his weight behind Republican candidates such as Representative Michael Sodrel of Indiana and Senator Rick Santorum in Pennsylvania who faced particularly difficult re-election battles (VandeHei 2006).

Why have some theorists challenged the candidate-centred perspective?

In recent years, the candidate-centred view of electoral politics has been challenged. An alternative view focuses upon the parties and their social bases. The parties have become increasingly 'European' in terms of alignment, insofar as the Republicans draw their support from white, traditionalist, conservative and wealthier communities and the Democrats are backed by those who are less affluent, liberals, as well as the racial and ethnic minority groups. Members of Congress belonging to the same party represent similar groups of people. They therefore tend to vote together, adopt broadly similar policies and stand on the basis of similar election platforms. The parties have become more homogeneous and polarised. Party loyalties have grown and the parties, rather than candidates, are the focus for mobilising the electorate.

Task 5.1

Should Congressional elections be seen as 'candidate-centred' or 'party-centred'?

Guidance

Although opinion has until recently stressed the candidate-centred character of US elections, the parties should not be disregarded.

- Despite the introduction of primaries, the parties can influence fundraising and the process of candidate selection.
- Voting trends are not as fluid as the 'candidate-centredness' school suggests. Despite talk of dealignment some decades ago, and suggestions that the electorate had become more volatile, voting is often based upon social groupings. African-Americans are loyal to the Democratic Party and most white evangelical Protestants back the Republicans.

What are the defining characteristics of Congressional elections?

Congressional elections have different dynamics from presidential contests. They are often fought on district, or statewide, rather than national issues. In a celebrated comment, a former Speaker of the House of Representatives, Tip O'Neill, said 'All politics is local.' Nonetheless, national politics do intrude. Party resources are committed to close races. In the November 2006 mid-term elections, both party hierarchies devoted large-scale resources to the Senate races in states such as Pennsylvania, Missouri and Tennessee. They played a part in determining who would be selected as candidate and then structured the character of the campaign.

The re-election of incumbents

Most Congressional contests are *uncompetitive* (see Figure 5.1). In other words, there is little doubt about the outcome and a particular candidate is assured of victory. In particular, incumbents are almost always re-elected. Even in November 1994, the year of the Republican 'revolution' when the party won control of both Congressional chambers and the Democrats suffered a major defeat, 90% of those seeking re-election to the House were returned. Incumbency rates are rather lower for the Senate, although this is partly because only a third of the Senate faces an election every 2 years and just one or two defeats have a significant impact on the statistics (see Figure 5.2).

Almost all the competitive contests are in 'open seats' where there is no incumbent. Furthermore, only some of these are seriously competitive. An open seat in a neighbourhood where large numbers are drawn from the ethnic and

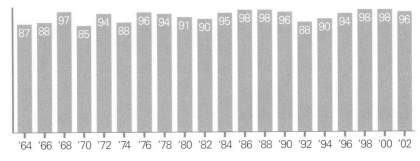

Source: OpenSecrets (2006a)

Figure 5.1 US House re-election rates, 1964–2002 (%)

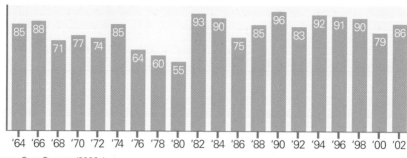

Source: OpenSecrets (2006a)

Figure 5.2 US Senate re-election rates, 1964–2002 (%)

racial minority groups will almost certainly be won by a Democratic candidate. An open seat in a rural or predominantly white area will probably fall to the Republicans. Table 5.1 shows the proportion of House seats beween 1990 and 2004 that can be considered 'open'.

Table 5.1 House elections, 1990–2004

Election year	Competitive House races (winner gains less than 55% of the vote)	% of House races
1990	57	13.1
1992	111	25.5
1994	98	22.5
1996	94	21.6
1998	47	10.8
2000	57	13.1
2002	47	10.8
2004	32	7.4

Source: adapted from Cook (2006)

Why are incumbents generally re-elected?

Funding

The reasons include the 'franking privilege' (whereby members of Congress can send mailings to constituents free of charge) and name recognition. However, there are more significant considerations. Most financial contributions are given to incumbents. This is for two principal reasons. First, campaign contributions can often provide a degree of access to a member of Congress. Second, there is also an expectation that the incumbent will win again and a donation therefore represents a worthwhile 'investment'.

Table 5.1 shows that the proportion of competitive seats has fallen signifi-cantly. Many more races are now foregone conclusions even when a party is relatively unpopular. Tables 5.2 and 5.3 show that incumbents attract a large proportion of campaign contributions.

Table 5.2 Senate elections, 2002

Type of candidate	Total raised	Number of candidates	Average raised
Incumbent	$191,520,090	33	$5,803,639
Challenger	$71,945,307	71	$1,013,314
Open seat	$106,411,603	42	$2,533,610
Grand total	$369,877,000	146	$2,533,404

Table 5.3 House of Representatives elections, 2002

Type of candidate	Total raised	Number of candidates	Average raised
Incumbent	$379,117,215	422	$898,382
Challenger	$96,037,295	486	$197,608
Open seat	$162,659,152	391	$416,008
Grand total	$637,813,662	1,299	$491,004

Source: OpenSecrets (2006a)

As Table 5.4 shows, political action committee (PAC) contributions to candidates are, in particular, directed towards incumbents.

Table 5.4 PAC contributions to Congressional candidates, 2002

Sector	Total (millions)	To incumbents (%)	To challengers (%)	To open seats (%)
Agribusiness	$77.7	83	6	11
Communication/ electronics	$75.0	89	2	9
Construction	$40.2	76	8	16
Defence	$12.3	91	2	7
Energy/natural resources	$129.6	82	3	14
Finance/insurance/ real estate	$174.7	85	3	12
Health	$207.9	83	4	13

Table 5.4 continued

Sector	Total (millions)	To incumbents (%)	To challengers (%)	To open seats (%)
Lawyers and lobbyists	$37.7	81	5	14
Transportation	$112.5	85	3	12
Miscellaneous business	$234.6	78	6	16
Labour	$301.3	70	12	19
Ideology/single issue	$188.2	50	18	32

Source: based on OpenSecrets (2006a)

Access to information

At the same time, while incumbents attract the bulk of the contributions, challengers are held back by the unintended consequences of federal law. As Hal Furman (1997) has observed:

> No one with a real job can afford to spend two years panhandling for campaign donations of under $1,000. Members of Congress who typically work three days a week, eight months a year (okay, I'm being generous) spend vast amounts of their time (actually our time) begging for contributions. Challengers, who more likely than not have to earn a living, don't have this luxury. Incumbents always complain about the time they spend fund raising but nothing ever changes.

Box 5.3

The perks of power

...In one of the lesser-known perks of power on Capitol Hill, lawmakers are using taxpayer-funded databases to cultivate constituents more attentively than ever. (Steve) Chabot — a six-term legislator from Cincinnati who finds himself imperiled this year after years of easy races — has a list of e-mail addresses of people who are most interested in tax cuts. His office recently hit the send button on a personal message to alert them to the congressman's support for extending tax breaks on dividends and capital gains...lawmakers are using the latest 'micro-targeting' techniques in their official communications...

'A major reason fewer incumbents lose is we have perfected the use of information technology,' said Rep. Barney Frank (D-Mass.). 'As incumbents, we have unlimited access to the most up-to-date technology in the world free of charge' he said...

Chabot is an illustration of the way lawmakers settle into their seats. He won by campaigning against then-President Bill Clinton's tax increases in 1994, taking 56 percent of the vote. He had tight races in 1996 and 1998. But after the 2000 census, Ohio's Republican governor and the GOP-led state legislature made life easier for him.

Box 5.3 (continued)

His new district was shaped to include more Republican neighborhoods. In an interview, Chabot said he estimates the new lines added about five percentage points to his November returns...

Like all incumbents, he has some important tools in knowing his district, ones not easily replicated by challengers trying to reach the roughly 600,000 people who live in a typical congressional district.

One of these tools is the congressional account each lawmaker can use to communicate with constituents. In the past, this money went mainly for sending newsletters or other mailings to voters, who often turned around and tossed them in the trash. But technology has allowed lawmakers to track the interests of individual voters, file the information into a database and then use e-mails or phone calls to engage directly with voters on issues they know they care about. In essence, this is the traditional 'franking' privilege updated — and made far more powerful — for the digital age...

Using taxpayers' money, legislators employ a new technology that allows them to call thousands of households simultaneously with a recorded message, asking people in their districts to join in on a conference call with their representative. With the push of a button, the constituent is on the line with the House member — and often 1,000 or more fellow constituents. More important, the lawmaker knows from the phone numbers where the respondents live and, from what they say on the call, what issues interest them.

...in January, Rep. Daniel E. Lungren (R-Calif.) briefed Republicans on how to host these tele-town halls using their office budget, participants said. Information gathered from the events, as well as e-mails and phone calls from constituents, gets plugged into a database, giving the incumbent something a challenger could only dream of: a detailed list of the specific interests of thousands of would-be voters. E-mail then allows for personal interaction — and a free reminder of why the incumbent should be reelected.

VandeHei and Babington (2006)

Redistricting

There are other reasons why incumbents, particularly those in the House of Representatives, are likely to be re-elected. Every 10 years, following the *reapportionment* process in the wake of the census, the number of House members allocated to each state is subject to reallocation. In the long run, the 'rustbelt' states of the northeast have lost Congressional seats, while states in the southwest (that have experienced the greatest population growth) have gained additional seats.

Reapportionment is followed by *redistricting*. (In some states, there is also the opportunity for redistricting at other points in the decade.) States redraw their electoral maps so that there are new or changed Congressional districts. In some states, including New Jersey and Pennsylvania, this is the responsibility of a 'non-partisan' commission. In many states, however, redistricting is in the hands of the state legislature. Over and over again, observers charge, the party controlling the legislature draws the map to protect its own incumbents. A Republican-controlled legislature would, for example, aid its incumbents by redrawing districts to include areas likely to back them. Solidly white neighbourhoods or rural communities might be added to the district to bolster the Republican majority. At the same time, the opposing party's 'natural' supporters can be concentrated together in a relatively small number of Congressional districts to minimise the number of seats that it wins. The process is sometimes dubbed 'cracking and packing'. Others talk about 'gerrymandering' (after Massachusetts Governor Elbridge Gerry, who in 1812 established a district so contorted that it resembled a salamander).

The redistricting process has been at its most controversial in Texas. It not only protected incumbents but seemed to advance partisan interests. In 2003, the Republican-controlled legislature sought to redistrict. Former House of Representatives Majority Leader Tom DeLay was believed to be responsible. Whereas previously Texas had been represented by 17 Democratic and 15 Republican members of Congress, the plan created 10 districts that would, it seemed, be overwhelmingly Democratic (all are majority black or Latino) and 22 districts that appeared to be solidly Republican (and were predominantly white). As Figure 5.3 shows, many of these districts appeared to have no geographical or social rationale.

In response, Democratic members from the two houses of the legislature attempted to prevent it from meeting and agreeing the redistricting plan by leaving for neighbouring Oklahoma and New Mexico. For a period, they made the legislature inquorate. (A quorum is the minimum number of members who have to be present if a meeting is to take place.)

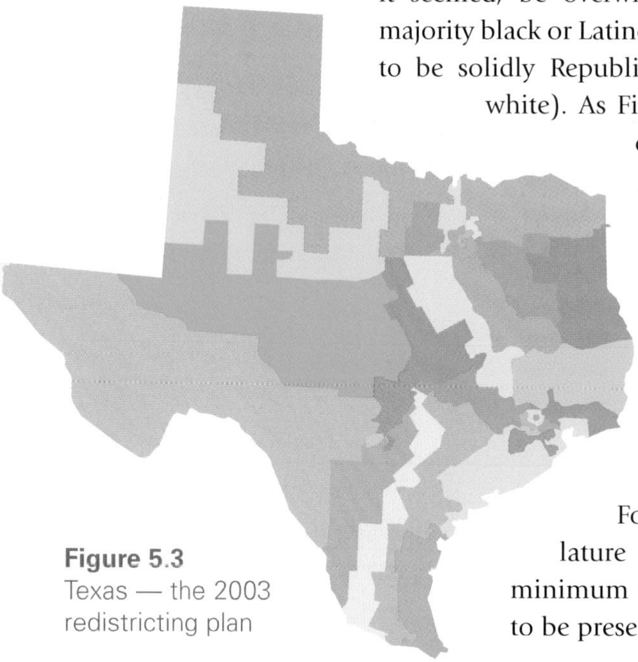

Figure 5.3
Texas — the 2003 redistricting plan

A subsequent appeal against the redistricting plan to the US Supreme Court failed. In November 2004, the Republicans won seven further seats across the USA. Five of these were in Texas and have been attributed to the redistricting process.

Box 5.4

The Texas gerrymander

Texas's 2003 redistricting was an extreme case of partisan gerrymandering…when Republicans took control of the state government, they decided to do a highly unusual second redistricting. Democratic state legislators protested and fled the state to deny the Republicans a quorum. But Texas eventually adopted a plan that tilted the state's delegation even further in the Republicans' favor…The Texas plan should be struck down on that ground, and because it violates the principle of one person one vote. More than a million people were added to the Texas population between the census and the 2003 redistricting…The state used outdated 2000 population data to draw the 2003 lines, producing districts that failed to give all of the state's voters equal representation in Congress…Partisan gerrymandering should be a bipartisan issue because both parties have been hurt by it and no doubt will be again. Its real victims, though, are the voters…If the Supreme Court permits those drawing legislative lines to use high-powered computers to create district lines that predetermine the outcomes of all but a handful of Congressional races, America may need to come up with another word for its form of government, because 'democracy' will hardly apply.

The New York Times, 1 March 2006

The politically charged methods that states use to draw Congressional districts are under attack by citizens groups, state legislators and the governor of California, all of whom are concerned that increasingly sophisticated map drawing has created a class of entrenched incumbents, stifled electoral competition and caused governmental gridlock.

Box 5.5

Arnie objects

Largely uncoordinated campaigns stretching from California to Massachusetts are pushing to end, or at least minimize, a time-honored staple of American politics: lawmakers drawing Congressional and legislative district maps in geographically convoluted ways to ensure the re-election of an incumbent or the dominance of a party.

Last month, Gov. Arnold Schwarzenegger of California, a state that has historically been at the forefront of political reform movements, proposed putting retired judges in

---

> ### Box 5.5 (continued)
>
> charge of redistricting, taking it out of the hands of the Legislature. Common Cause, one of the nonpartisan groups championing changes in the system, said campaigns to overhaul redistricting were under way in at least eight states, including California, Colorado, Florida, Georgia, Maryland, Massachusetts, Pennsylvania and Rhode Island.
>
> The increased attention to the issue is in part due to the effectiveness of efforts in 2003 in Texas, where Republicans, with the backing of the White House, forced through a midterm redistricting that effectively cost four Texas Democrats their seats. The complaints are also spurred by the way computers and the enormous amount of available voting data have turned redistricting into a surgically precise procedure and opened up to anyone with a laptop what was once dominated by legislative tacticians with decades of knowledge.
>
> Nagourney (2005)

> ### Box 5.6
> **Legal upholding of redistricting**
>
> The Supreme Court on Wednesday rejected a broad challenge to Texas's controversial Congressional redistricting plan, giving a victory to the Republican Party and the architect of the plan, Tom DeLay, the former House majority leader.
>
> But at the same time, the court ruled that the Texas Legislature violated the Voting Rights Act in redrawing a particular district in southwestern Texas when it adopted the plan in 2003. The Legislature had carved up Laredo, removing 100,000 Mexican-Americans and adding an Anglo population from the Hill Country to shore up the faltering prospects of the Republican incumbent…The ruling also cleared the way for other states to join Texas in adopting the approach that was challenged in the case: setting aside the tradition of redrawing Congressional districts only after the once-a-decade census, instead using a change of political control in the state governments as reason to reshape their maps.
>
> Greenhouse (2006)

Other reasons why incumbents are re-elected

There are other reasons why incumbents almost always secure re-election:
(1) The 'franking privilege' allows members of Congress to send post to their constituents without paying postage. They can use this to publicise and promote their efforts on behalf of the district or state. Challengers must use campaign funds to send their mailings.

(2) Congressional offices are well staffed. A senator or member of the House will not only have secretarial and administrative staff but also caseworkers who can devote time and attention to addressing constituent problems.

(3) Incumbents often have a relatively high profile in the local and state-based media. In some cases, they attract national attention, and this gives them name recognition.

(4) Long-serving members of Congress may gain important Committees, assignments and projects. This provides further visibility and may enable an incumbent to shape policy in the interests of the state or district.

(5) Incumbents can attach 'riders' to legislation or secure 'earmarks' to gain funding for projects in their home district or state. The process by which members of Congress seek funding and sometimes make this a condition for backing legislation is traditionally dubbed 'pork-barrel politics' or more simply just 'pork'.

(6) Congressional Campaign Committees are able to raise significant amounts of funding. Although some will be assigned to seats that the parties hope to win, much is also allocated to incumbents, particularly those who have loyal voting records.

The Republicans may have an additional advantage in holding on to their seats. They have, as Peter Wallsten and Tom Hamburger emphasise, pioneered the application of marketing techniques to campaigning.

Box 5.7

Republican marketing tools

...the Republican Party still holds the lead in the art and science of obtaining power — and keeping it.

The fact is that over two or three decades, the GOP has painstakingly built up a series of structural advantages that make the party increasingly difficult to beat. And in the last five years, it has strengthened its hold under President Bush and his political guru, Karl Rove...The Republican fortress has many underpinnings, such as gerrymandered congressional districts that favor the GOP, an intellectual infrastructure that churns ideas through conservative think tanks and media, an ever-stronger political and policy-based alliance with corporate America, and the most sophisticated vote-tracking technology around.

Some of the GOP advantages are recent developments, such as the database called Voter Vault, which was used to precision in the San Diego County special election. The program allows ground-level party activists to track voters by personal hobbies, professional interests, geography — even by their favorite brands of toothpaste and soda and which gym they belong to.

> ### Box 5.7 (continued)
>
> Both parties can identify voters by precinct, address, party affiliation and, often, their views on hot-button issues. Democrats also use marketing data, but Voter Vault includes far more information culled from marketing sources — including retailers, magazine subscription services, even auto dealers — giving Republicans a high-tech edge in the kind of grass-roots politics that has long been the touchstone of Democratic activists.
>
> As a result, Republicans have moved well ahead of Democrats nationally in their ability to find previously unaffiliated voters or even wavering Democrats and to target them with specially tailored messages.
>
> Wallsten and Hamburger (2006)

Task 5.2

(a) Why are incumbents generally re-elected?

(b) Should redistricting be the responsibility of elected politicians?

Guidance

- The reasons why incumbents are re-elected include the 'franking privilege', name recognition, the pattern of financial contributions and the consequences of partisan redistricting.
- Many argue that redistricting should be the responsibility, as it is in some states, of an independent non-partisan commission. However, others contend that such commissions are unaccountable to the voter.

Race, redistricting and representation

Women and minority groups are under-represented in almost all national legislatures. The US Congress is no exception. Although minority representation has grown dramatically, half a century after the end of segregation Congress remains a largely white institution. Of the 435 members of the House of Representatives, 42 are members of the Congressional Black Caucus. In the Senate, there is just one African-American, Barack Obama, who was elected to represent Illinois in 2004.

In part, this arose because although many Congressional districts included significant minority populations, they were outnumbered by whites. There was a feeling that, in these districts where there was a problem of 'vote dilution', black candidates had little chance of success.

Some saw an answer to this in the creation of majority–minority districts. From 1982 onwards, when the Voting Rights Act was amended, some district boundaries were drawn to ensure that there was a black majority. This would, it was said, ensure that greater numbers of African-Americans were elected to Congress. The process did, however, require the creation of districts that had no geographical rationale or cohesion. Indeed, some had a bizarre shape. In 1993, in *Shaw* v *Reno*, the Supreme Court considered the constitutionality of a district in North Carolina. It was more than 160 miles in length and tied together different and unrelated pockets of the African–American population. Shaw and subsequent rulings (most notably *Miller* v *Johnson* in 1995) established that race could not be the 'predominant factor' in drawing up electoral districts.

Although the Court conceded that the process of drawing up districts could consider race if it was 'narrowly tailored to further a compelling governmental interest', it asserted that majority–minority districts violated the 14th Amendment, which guaranteed that all would be afforded 'equal protection of the laws'. Writing the majority opinion for the Court, Sandra Day O'Connor argued that racial classifications were 'by their very nature odious to a free people whose institutions are founded upon the doctrine of equality'. The creation of separate voting districts for African-Americans or Latinos, she warned, 'threatens to carry us further from the goal of a political system in which race no longer matters'.

The 'paradox' in Congressional electoral politics

There is a paradox in Congressional electoral politics. Although the public is critical of Congress as a whole and at times believes that it is untrustworthy, most people have confidence in, and give high approval ratings to, their own member of Congress. The reasons for this cannot be identified with any precision but almost certainly include the resources devoted to constituency casework and 'pork' (the securing of federally funded projects such as a road building plan that will bring employment or some other form of material assistance to the district or state). Therefore, in part, it can be explained by reference to the factors that determine the high re-election rate for incumbents. Members of Congress are almost always assiduous in dealing with individual problems facing their electorate and they have staff members in the district or state as well as in Washington DC who are ready to assist. 'Earmarks', furthermore, allow them to secure advantages for their constituents when federal government spending is allocated. As 'Tip' O'Neill (Speaker of the House of Representatives 1977–87) notes:

A politician learns that if a constituent calls about a problem, even if it's a streetlight out, you don't tell them to call City Hall. You call City Hall. Members of the House learn this quicker than anyone else because they only have a two-year term. They learn that if you don't pay attention to the voters, you soon will find yourself right back there with them.

Chapter 5

Task 5.3

Table 5.5 lists the results of a survey carried out in January 2006 by SurveyUSA. It shows the degree to which people back their own senators. If states are weighted on the basis of their population, 54% of those asked approve of their senator while 33% disapprove. Examine the table and answer the questions that follow.

Table 5.5   Changes in the US presidential nomination process

Rank	State	US senator	Party	Approve (%)	Disapprove (%)
1	ME	Snowe, Olympia	R	75	21
2	HI	Inouye, Daniel	D	73	19
3	ME	Collins, Susan	R	72	22
3	IL	Obama, Barack	D	72	20
5	AZ	McCain, John	R	71	26
5	RI	Reed, Jack	D	71	22
7	SD	Johnson, Tim	D	70	26
8	ND	Conrad, Kent	D	67	27
8	NE	Nelson, Ben	D	67	24
10	NM	Domenici, Pete	R	66	27
10	VT	Jeffords, James	Independent	66	28
10	WV	Rockefeller, Jay	D	66	28
10	AK	Stevens, Ted	R	66	29
14	WV	Byrd, Robert	D	65	31
14	IA	Grassley, Charles	R	65	29
14	VT	Leahy, Patrick	D	65	29
17	NY	Clinton, Hillary	D	64	32
17	ND	Dorgan, Byron	D	64	30
17	LA	Vitter, David	R	64	29
20	TX	Hutchison, Kay	R	63	24
20	CT	Lieberman, Joseph	D	63	30
20	MS	Lott, Trent	R	63	33
20	VA	Warner, John	R	63	25
24	DE	Carper, Thomas	D	62	29
24	UT	Hatch, Orrin	R	62	29
24	IN	Lugar, Richard	R	62	26
27	MA	Kennedy, Edward	D	61	34
28	MT	Baucus, Max	D	60	32
28	IN	Bayh, Evan	D	60	30

Task 5.3 (continued)

Rank	State	US senator	Party	Approve (%)	Disapprove (%)
28	SC	Graham, Lindsey	R	60	31
28	AR	Pryor, Mark	D	60	29
28	NY	Schumer, Charles	D	60	31
28	AL	Shelby, Richard	R	60	29
28	OR	Wyden, Ron	D	60	27
35	HI	Akaka, Daniel	D	59	31
35	NM	Bingaman, Jeff	D	59	28
35	MS	Cochran, Thad	R	59	33
35	NE	Hagel, Chuck	R	59	33
35	WI	Kohl, Herb	D	59	31
35	NV	Reid, Harry	D	59	38
35	WY	Thomas, Craig	R	59	31
35	SD	Thune, John	R	59	37
43	KS	Brownback, Sam	R	58	32
43	CT	Dodd, Christopher	D	58	32
43	NH	Gregg, Judd	R	58	31
43	AR	Lincoln, Blanche	D	58	32
43	MD	Mikulski, Barbara	D	58	34
43	AL	Sessions, Jeff	R	58	30
49	UT	Bennett, Robert	R	57	27
49	DE	Biden, Joseph	D	57	38
49	ID	Craig, Larry	R	57	30
49	WY	Enzi, Michael	R	57	31
49	PA	Specter, Arlen	R	57	37
54	VA	Allen, George	R	56	29
54	LA	Landrieu, Mary	D	56	40
56	MO	Bond, Kit	R	55	36
56	MN	Coleman, Norm	R	55	36
56	ID	Crapo, Michael	R	55	29
56	MA	Kerry, John	D	55	39
56	CO	Salazar, Ken	D	55	34
61	NC	Dole, Elizabeth	R	54	35
61	WI	Feingold, Russell	D	54	38
61	IA	Harkin, Tom	D	54	39
64	WA	Cantwell, Maria	D	53	34
64	RI	Chafee, Lincoln	R	53	38

Task 5.3 (continued)

Rank	State	US senator	Party	Approve (%)	Disapprove (%)
64	MI	Levin, Carl	D	53	34
64	AK	Murkowski, Lisa	R	53	40
64	WA	Murray, Patty	D	53	39
64	FL	Nelson, Bill	D	53	29
64	KS	Roberts, Pat	R	53	35
71	TN	Alexander, Lamar	R	52	36
71	SC	DeMint, Jim	R	52	34
71	IL	Durbin, Richard	D	52	34
71	CA	Feinstein, Dianne	D	52	38
71	KY	McConnell, Mitch	R	52	37
71	NH	Sununu, John	R	52	36
77	GA	Chambliss, Saxby	R	51	35
77	MN	Dayton, Mark	D	51	36
77	MD	Sarbanes, Paul	D	51	34
77	OR	Smith, Gordon	R	51	35
81	NV	Ensign, John	R	50	37
81	GA	Isakson, Johnny	R	50	36
81	MI	Stabenow, Debbie	D	50	35
81	MO	Talent, Jim	R	50	38
85	OK	Coburn, Tom	R	49	39
85	OK	Inhofe, James	R	49	38
85	OH	Voinovich, George	R	49	40
88	CO	Allard, Wayne	R	48	34
88	CA	Boxer, Barbara	D	48	39
88	NJ	Corzine, Jon	D	48	40
88	TN	Frist, Bill	R	48	43
92	OH	DeWine, Mike	R	47	41
93	TX	Cornyn, John	R	46	31
94	NC	Burr, Richard	R	44	35
94	AZ	Kyl, Jon	R	44	39
94	PA	Santorum, Rick	R	44	46
97	KY	Bunning, Jim	R	43	44
97	FL	Martinez, Mel	R	43	42
99	MT	Burns, Conrad	R	42	51
100	NJ	Lautenberg, Frank	D	40	44

Source: adapted from SurveyUSA (2006)

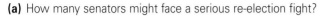

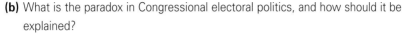

Task 5.3 (continued)

(a) How many senators might face a serious re-election fight?

(b) What is the paradox in Congressional electoral politics, and how should it be explained?

Guidance

- Those with an approval rating of about 54% or under may face difficulties, although much will also depend upon prevailing political trends and demographic shifts in and out of the state.
- Although Congress is not (collectively) held in high regard, residents in a particular district or state are generally supportive of their own member or Senator. In part, it can be explained by reference to the factors that determine the high re-election rate for incumbents.

'Running scared'

Although incumbents are almost certain to be re-elected, members of Congress do not always see it in these terms. Their anxiety about the possibility of losing provides a further reason why they will probably keep winning their seat as they 'run scared'. In a description of a teaching session on this subject, Jeffrey Bernstein spells out the way in which he explains this to students.

> Members of Congress 'run scared.' Even in the absence of any reason to fear for their electoral lives, they worry incessantly about losing the next election. This keeps them risk averse and keeps their behavior in line with what they perceive their constituents want.

> a. I always take my 100 person lecture class and have them all pretend they are members of Congress. Ninety-five percent of them will be reelected, so they all have little reason to fear. Then, I randomly call out names of five who lost. I encourage all of them to look around the room at those who lost. People who lose are not just statistics — they may include the person I eat lunch with, the woman with an office down the hall from mine, the man who serves on my committee with me. When people see how defeat can touch those close to them, they get a little more paranoid about losing.

> b. I remind students also that while defeat in any given year is rare, more members leave office due to electoral defeat than any other reason (such as retirement). It is true that most members are likely to win any given election, a long congressional career requires stringing along a large number of wins. This is not always easy.

Task 5.4

Why do members of Congress 'run scared', and how does it affect their behaviour?

Chapter 5

Task 5.4 (continued)

Guidance

Bernstein suggests the numbers who fail to secure re-election are small, but that they are felt at a personal level within the Congressional 'community'. Furthermore, elections to the House of Representatives are frequent. Therefore, members have to think about the risk of loss (however small) on a daily basis. Senators and members of the House ensure that they pay close attention to their constituents. This inevitably weakens the hold of the parties and other collective structures within Congress.

Contesting an open seat or challenging a weak incumbent

Although crucially important, incumbency is not destiny. Incumbents are sometimes defeated in either primary contests or the general election. Some open seats also offer opportunities. What other factors determine electoral success for both incumbents and successful challengers?

Finance

Financial resources play a significant role. In the 2000 race for a New Jersey Senate seat, Jon Corzine, the Democrats' candidate, spent over $60 million. Of this, $3 million was spent on election day itself in an effort to maximise turnout among Democratic supporters. Much of this was Corzine's own money. However, financial resources do not assure success. Although Corzine won, he secured only 51% of the poll. In the 2000 New York Senate race, Republican Rick Lazio spent $7 million more than the Democratic candidate (Hillary Clinton) but lost by a wide margin.

Coat-tails effect

In presidential election years, there may be a 'coat-tails effect'. If there is a strong presidential candidate, voters may back Congressional candidates from the same party. Put another way, there is a reduction in 'split-ticket voting'. This refers to voters who back candidates from different parties on the same election day. They may, for example, support a Republican presidential candidate, but back the Democrats at Congressional and state level. Table 5.6 can be used to assess the extent to which there has been a coat-tails effect in particular elections.

Table 5.6 Net change in the position of the winning presidential candidate's party

Election year	Winning presidential candidate	Party	House of Representatives	Senate
1976	Jimmy Carter	D	+1	0
1980	Ronald Reagan	R	+34	+12
1984	Ronald Reagan	R	+15	−1
1988	George H. W. Bush	R	−2	0
1992	Bill Clinton	D	−18	+1
1996	Bill Clinton	D	+9	−2
2000	George W. Bush	R	−1	−4
2004	George W. Bush	R	+4	+4

Source: adapted from English (2003), p. 33

Timing

In mid-term elections, it is usual for the president's party to lose seats. This may be because there is a degree of disillusionment with his party comparable with the by-election losses that a governing party often suffers in the UK. There are, however, exceptions. In 1998, the Democrats made gains although Bill Clinton occupied the White House. Some suspected that this was because the Republicans had over-reached themselves in their handling of his impeachment and subsequent trial by the Senate.

Task 5.5

What is the 'coat-tails effect' and how significant a role does it play in Congressional elections?

Guidance
- President Ronald Reagan is often cited when the 'coat-tails effect' is discussed. Reaganism rested upon a coalition of voters that attracted significant numbers of Democrats (sometimes dubbed 'Reagan Democrats'). White, male manual workers were, in particular, drawn by Reagan's resolute anti-communism, his commitment to law and order, and his social conservatism.
- Later winning presidential candidates had small or negligible 'coat-tails'. The reasons for this may include the character of their candidacies and the failure of later Republicans (with the partial exception of George W. Bush in 2004) to convey an image of resolution and 'toughness'.

The role of technology

Former Vermont Governor Howard Dean's use of the internet for fundraising, the rallying of supporters (through campaign blogs), and for online polls, has already been noted (see p. 20). As the 2006 mid-term elections approached, the internet and mobile phone technology seemed to be playing even more of a role.

Both Democrats and Republicans increased their use of e-mail, interactive websites, blogs, podcasts and text messaging to raise funds, organise get-out-the-vote efforts and ensure a credible turnout at campaign rallies. The internet has proved to be much more cost efficient than knocking on doors and making telephone calls.

There is a large audience for web activity. According to the Pew Research Center, 29% of people went online as the 2004 elections approached. By 2006, 50 million Americans were going to the internet for news every day. Seventy percent of the population have access to the internet.

Much internet activity is protected by the 1st Amendment to the US Constitution and is unregulated. In March 2006, the Federal Election Commission confirmed that blogs and other internet commentaries were unrestricted. Only paid political advertisements are restricted. Campaigns buying such advertisements must use 'hard' money that is limited and regulated by federal election campaign law.

The use of the internet has become more markedly negative. Some campaigns use 'viral attack videos' directed against an opponent. They are not overtly associated with the candidate or campaign but are instead designed for distribution by e-mail chains. There is evidence that both parties have established websites to discredit other candidates. According to Adam Nagourney of *The New York Times*, Republicans in Tennessee created www.fancyford.com. This attacked the 'lavish' spending habits of Republican Representative Harold E. Ford Jr. and drew 100,000 hits the first weekend. Websites such as this can have a 'multiplier' effect by attracting extensive press coverage.

There are, however, limits upon the scope and the impact of internet campaigning. The internet is used to a lesser extent by those aged over 65 (who are most likely to vote). It is also used more heavily by people on middle and upper-level incomes although the socioeconomic 'gap' is diminishing. Perhaps more importantly, most computer users surf between websites and may also be undertaking other activities at the same time. A website may therefore have less impact than a television advertisement or a campaign mailshot.

The campaigns are already thinking about the ways in which they can utilise new and developing forms of technology. In particular, they are considering the beaming of video advertisements to mobile phones.

Task 5.6

(a) How big an impact has the internet had upon campaigning?

(b) Has internet campaigning had a positive or negative impact upon the electoral process?

Guidance

You might consider the following points when answering these questions:

- The internet is displacing traditional forms of communication between a campaign and the voter.
- Some suggest that the internet is creating new forms of community and offering new mechanisms (such as online polling) for direct democracy. Others point to the opportunities that it offers for unchecked and unaccountable campaigning. It is easy to destroy a reputation through negative coverage and comment. However, this argument can in turn be countered. The blogging community has to some extent 'policed' the activities of the campaigns by exposing underhand forms of activity.

Results of the 2006 mid-term elections

Although there had been predictions in the weeks preceding the 2006 mid-term elections that the Democrats would take the House of Representatives and perhaps the Senate (although this had seemed less likely), some of the assumptions that had been made by commentators about elections and voting behaviour in the preceding years had to be modified. In the 2004 presidential contest, voting loyalties seemed be entrenched. There was extensive talk of 'polarisation' and much of the country seemed split between highly committed Democrats and highly committed Republicans. In addition, many House Republicans seemed protected by the redistricting process, which had ensured that their seats were safe from serious challenge. Furthermore, because incumbents, if standing, are almost certain to be re-elected (see 'What are the defining characteristics of Congressional elections?' on p. 73) the Democrats appeared to be facing an uphill task.

Nevertheless, the Democrats won control of both the House of Representatives and, albeit much more narrowly, the Senate (see Tables 5.7 and 5.8).

Table 5.7 House of Representatives

Party	2006 total	2004 total
Republicans	202	232
Democrats	233	202
Independents	0	1

| Table 5.8 | Senate |

Party	2006 total	2004 total
Republicans	49	55
Democrats	51	44
Independents	0	0

Notes: the 2006 figure for the Democrats includes Joseph Lieberman (Connecticut) who had run as an independent following his defeat in the Democratic primary and Bernie Sanders of Vermont, a longstanding left-leaning independent. Both were pledged to 'caucus' with the Democrats and ensure that the party had control over the Senate. Although all the members of the House of Representatives face elections every 2 years, senators serve 6-year terms. Only a third of the Senate seats are contested at each election.

The scale of the shift should not be exaggerated. Although both chambers changed hands, only limited numbers of seats changed hands, (see Tables 5.7 and 5.8). Incumbency continued to play a pivotal role in shaping election outcomes. Ninety-four percent of incumbents seeking re-election to the House of Representatives were returned (OpenSecrets 2006b). This was only slightly down from 2002 and 2004 when 96% and 98% of House incumbents were returned. In the Senate (where because of the small number of seats being contested a single loss makes a significant difference in percentage terms) 79% of senators seeking re-election in 2006 were victorious. This compared with 86% and 96% in 2002 and 2004 (OpenSecrets 2006c).

Established voting patterns were, broadly speaking, maintained. Seventy percent of white evangelicals (one of the most conservative demographic groupings) voted Republican. 60% of those who attended church more regularly than once a week (a grouping that includes members of other denominations apart from those attached to the evangelical churches) backed the Republicans. The gender gap narrowed, but 53% of white men supported Republican candidates compared with 50% of white women. In contrast to the white electorate, voters drawn from the African-American, Latino and Asian-American minorities overwhelmingly backed the Democrats.

Despite these continuities, the significance of the 2006 mid-term elections should not be underestimated. The Republicans 'lock' on Congress that had been maintained (except for an 18-month period in 2001–03 when the Democrats had the narrowest of majorities in the Senate following the defection of a Republican) was ended. A significant proportion of Republicans stayed at home. More importantly, a clear majority of independents (who despite the talk just 2 years earlier of polarisation constituted 26% of the voters) backed the Democrats. Fifty-seven percent voted for a Democratic candidate, while only 39% supported the Republicans. Why did this happen?

- Traditionally, Congressional politics are 'local' in character. Voters consider the issues and interests associated with their home state or district. In 2006, however, just 34% of voters said that local issues mattered most to them. Sixty percent pointed to national concerns.

- The elections were, in significant part, a 'referendum' on the policies pursued by the Bush administration and the Congressional Republicans. Whereas 22% said that they voted so as to show support for President Bush, 36% wanted to oppose the president. Furthermore, many more had concerns about administration policies that led them to back the Democrats or stay at home.
- In particular, the Iraq war took its toll on the Republican vote. Sixty-seven percent said that Iraq was either 'extremely' or 'very' important to them. A clear majority of the voters disapproved of the war.
- Other issues also hurt the Republicans. Significant majorities stressed the importance of ethical issues and corruption. Memories of the Jack Abramoff scandal, claims that lobbyists had 'bought' members of Congress and rewarded them for particular votes were fresh in many voters' minds. Half the voters believed, despite some encouraging statistics, that the US economy was either 'not good' or in 'poor' condition.
- These specific concerns were tied to overall perceptions of the Bush administration and the state of the country. Just 12% of voters were 'enthusiastic' about the president. Clear majorities disapprove of his record. Furthermore, when asked whether the USA was 'going in the right direction' (a question often regarded by commentators as a bellwether that can be used to predict election outcomes), 55% said 'no'. (All these figures are for exit polls of voters in contests for the House of Representatives; source: adapted from CNN, 2006.)

Table 5.9   2006 mid-term elections — exit poll (voting for the House of Representatives)

Vote by gender

Total (%)	Democrat (%)	Republican (%)
Male (49)	50	47
Female (51)	55	43

Vote by race

Total (%)	Democrat (%)	Republican (%)
White (79)	47	51
African-American (10)	89	10
Latino (8)	69	30
Asian (2)	62	37
Other (2)	55	42

Vote by age

Total (%)	Democrat (%)	Republican (%)
18–29 (12)	60	38
30–44 (24)	53	45
45 59 (34)	53	46
60 and older (29)	50	48

Vote by income

Total (%)	Democrat (%)	Republican (%)
Under $15,000 (7)	67	30
$15,000–30,000 (12)	61	36
$30,000–50,000 (21)	56	43
$50,000–75,000 (22)	50	48
$75,000–100,000 (16)	52	47
$100,000–150,000 (13)	47	51
$150,000–200,000 (5)	47	51
$200,000 or more (5)	45	53

Vote by education

Total (%)	Democrat (%)	Republican (%)
No high school (3)	64	35
High-school graduate (21)	55	44
Some college (31)	51	47
College graduate (27)	49	49
Postgraduate (18)	58	41

Vote by religion

Total (%)	Democrat (%)	Republican (%)
Protestant (55)	44	54
Catholic (26)	55	44
Jewish (2)	87	12
Other (6)	71	25
None (11)	74	22

Are you married?

Total (%)	Democrat (%)	Republican (%)
Yes (68)	48	51
No (32)	64	34

How George W. Bush is handling his job

Total (%)	Democrat (%)	Republican (%)
Strongly approve (19)	9	90
Somewhat approve (23)	18	79
Somewhat disapprove (15)	59	38
Strongly disapprove (41	91	7

Family's financial situation

Total (%)	Democrat (%)	Republican (%)
Better (30)	28	71
Worse (25)	77	20
Same (44)	56	42

Importance of Iraq

Total (%)	Democrat (%)	Republican (%)
Extremely important (35)	60	39
Very important (32)	46	52
Somewhat important (21)	47	50
Not at all important (10)	62	36

Importance of terrorism

Total (%)	Democrat (%)	Republican (%)
Extremely important (39)	46	53
Very important (33)	51	47
Somewhat important (20)	65	32
Not at all important (6)	66	31

Importance of economy

Total (%)	Democrat (%)	Republican (%)
Extremely important (39)	59	39
Very important (43)	48	50
Somewhat important (49)	49	48
Not at all important (3)	55	42

Importance of illegal immigration

Total (%)	Democrat (%)	Republican (%)
Extremely important (30)	46	52
Very important (32)	49	50
Somewhat important (29)	61	37
Not at all important (8)	66	31

Chapter 5

Importance of value issues

Total (%)	Democrat (%)	Republican (%)
Extremely important (36)	40	58
Very important (21)	51	48
Somewhat important (20)	61	37
Not at all important (22)	69	29

Importance of corruption/ethics

Total (%)	Democrat (%)	Republican (%)
Extremely important (41)	59	39
Very important (33)	51	47
Somewhat important (18)	46	52
Not at all important (7)	43	55

Vote by size of community

Total (%)	Democrat (%)	Republican (%)
Big cities (10)	68	30
Smaller cities (20)	57	41
Suburbs (47)	50	48
Small towns (5)	49	48
Rural (18)	48	51

Vote by region

Total (%)	Democrat (%)	Republican (%)
Northeast (22)	63	35
Midwest (27)	52	47
South (30)	45	53
West (21)	54	43

Source: adapted from CNN (2006)

Task 5.7

What other conclusions, apart from those discussed above, can be drawn from the 2006 exit poll?

Guidance

Look first at the proportion of poll respondents who are drawn from a particular grouping (such as those from the south) or who answer a question in a particular way

Task 5.7 (continued)

(e.g. those who 'strongly support' President Bush). Then consider whether there is a correlation between these categories and the way in which votes are cast. Are southerners more likely to back Democratic or Republican candidates? Which way do unmarried people 'lean'? What about those who see illegal immigration as an 'extremely important' issue?

Further reading and references

- Bernstein, J. 'What high school government teachers should know about Congressional elections', *CongressLink*, www.congresslink.org/print_expert_congressionalelections.htm
- CNN (2006) *US House of Representatives/National/Exit Poll*, www.cnn.com/ELECTION/2006/pages/results/states/US/H/00/epolls.0.html
- Cook, R. (2006) 'Democrats Made Gains in All Regions of the Country', Pew Research Centre, 14 November, http://pewresearch.org/obdeck/?ObDeckID=90
- Crowley, M. (2006) 'Party crasher: Katherine Harris won't go away', *The New Republic*, 6 March.
- English, R. (2003) *The United States Congress*, Manchester University Press.
- Furman, H. (1997) 'Why incumbents rarely lose', *Online Nevada*, vol. 5, no. 1, http://nj.npri.org/nj97/01/why.htm
- Greenhouse, L. (2006) 'Justices uphold most remapping in Texas by GOP', *The New York Times*, 29 June.
- Nagourney, A. (2005) 'States see growing campaign to change redistricting laws', *The New York Times*, 7 February.
- Nagourney, A. (2006) 'Internet injects sweeping change into US politics', *The New York Times*, 2 April.
- OpenSecrets (2006a) *The Big Picture — 2002 Cycle: Reelection Rates Over the Years*
- OpenSecrets (2006b) *2006 Election Analysis: Incumbents Linked to Corruption Lose, but Money Still Wins*, www.opensecrets.org/pressreleases/2006/PostElection.11.8.asp.
- OpenSecrets (2006c) *Reelection Rates Over the Years*, www.opensecrets.org/bigpicture/reelect.asp?Cycle=2004&chamb=H and www.opensecrets.org/bigpicture/reelect.asp?Cycle=2004&chamb=S
- Slevin, P. (2006) 'After war injury, an Iraq vet takes on politics', *Washington Post*, 19 February.
- Stonecash, J. M., Brewer, M. D. and Mariani, M. D. (2003) *Diverging Parties: Social Change, Realignment, and Party Polarization*, Westview Press.

- SurveyUSA (2006) *Approval ratings for all 100 US senators as of 1/26/06*, www.surveyusa.com
- Urbina, I. (2006) 'Popular Ohio Democrat drops out of race, and perhaps politics', *The New York Times*, 14 February.
- VandeHei, J. (2006) 'Bush shows strategy for keeping Hill majorities: Democrats assailed on national security, as well as the economy', *Washington Post*, 25 March.
- VandeHei, J. and Babington, C. (2006) 'Technology Sharpens the Incumbents' Edge: Redistricting Also Complicates Democrats' Effort to Take Control of House', *Washington Post*, 7 June, A01, www.washingtonpost.com/wp-dyn/content/article/2006/06/06/AR2006060601330.html
- Wallsten, P. and Hamburger, T. (2006) 'The GOP knows you don't like anchovies', *Los Angeles Times*, 25 June.

Who votes which way, and why?

Chapter 6 considers voting behaviour. It looks at the short-term and long-term variables that inform voting decisions as well as the issues and campaigns that may shape electoral outcomes.

Fixed loyalties?

Although most reports and commentaries focus on election issues and personalities, and scholarly studies that at least in the 1980s talked of partisan dealignment, voting behaviour is largely shaped by long-term variables. Despite the intensity of the media coverage, the tensions that can often accompany election battles, the costs that are entailed and the sustained efforts to win voters across, significant numbers of voters have fixed voting loyalties. They may have doubts or reservations but, if they cast a vote, it will be for candidates belonging to the same party. Indeed, many will 'inherit' their parents' attitudes, attachments and 'partisanship'. Despite surface appearance, election campaigns are therefore only, in part, an attempt to win the backing of those undecided 'floating voters'. Just as importantly, they are directed towards ensuring a high level of turnout among groupings thought to be loyal to the party. What are the long-term variables that shape and structure voting loyalties? They include race and ethnicity, gender and socioeconomic status. Religious faith and region are also important.

However, some people do change their opinions over time. Those who are married and go on to have children tend to see issues differently from those who are single (although those who get married may have had different attitudes from their early days and so the 'marriage effect' may be smaller than it appears at first). Parents will be concerned about their children's upbringing and may well attach greater importance to 'moral' issues and security concerns than those who have yet to have children. The personality of the candidate (or at least the ways in which he or she is represented and projected) is also a consideration.

Furthermore, issues aside, incumbency is a significant factor in US Congressional and state-based elections. Regardless of earlier preferences, significant numbers of people vote to re-elect the incumbent. Once elected,

many public officials continue to serve until they die or choose to retire. Relatively few incumbents are defeated, even in electoral landslides such as in 1994.

US political scientists often begin studies of voting behaviour by considering partisanship.

What is partisanship, and how does it shape voting behaviour?

Partisanship is the sense of identification with and attachment to a party. It is the most solid and reliable determinant of voting behaviour. This may sound self-evident. However, the US parties are much looser than the European political parties, and there is always a 'cross-over' vote. In other words, some Democrat supporters vote for a Republican president and some Republicans back a Democrat. Some regard the size of the cross-over vote as a measure of partisanship. If the cross-over vote is small, it suggests that there are strong partisan loyalties. If it is relatively large, it may be that partisan feelings are rather weak.

Table 6.1 shows the degree of support for the other party's presidential candidate by Democratic and Republican identifiers

Table 6.1 Partisan identification and the presidential vote, 1988–2004 (%)

	Bush (2004)	Kerry (2004)	Bush (2000)	Gore (2000)	Dole (1996)	Clinton (1996)	Bush (1992)	Clinton (1992)	Bush (1988)	Dukakis (1988)
Democrat	11	89	11	86	10	84	10	77	17	82
Republican	93	6	91	8	80	13	73	10	91	8

Source: adapted from CNN (2004)

How is partisanship 'transmitted'?

Scholars do not agree about the determinants of political socialisation. (Political socialisation refers to the ways in which people acquire political values and ideas. In many cases this will be a childhood experience.) Some, including Robert Hess and Judith Torney, have stressed the importance of the school system. Others such as Stanley Renshon and James C. Davies emphasise the importance of parents and the family: 'most of the individual's political personality — his tendencies to think and act politically in particular ways — have been determined at home' (Verba et al. 2003). Indeed, Richard Niemi and M. Kent Jennings (1991, pp. 970–88) argue that parental opinion remains a factor shaping voting decisions and attitudes towards particular issues even when children have become adults. In a separate study written with Franco Mattei, Niemi also argues that 'independent' parents, who have no party attachments, 'transmit' their political attitudes. Indeed, they suggest that independent opinions are transmitted more efficiently than partisanship (Mattei and Niemi 1991, pp. 161–74).

Task 6.1

(a) What are the principal determinants of partisanship?

(b) To what extent does partisan voting appear to have changed in character between the 1990s and 2000 onwards?

(c) Suggest reasons for any shift.

Guidance

- Most scholars argue that partisanship is 'inherited' from an individual's parents.
- However, looking beyond the agencies of political socialisation, it is shaped by long-term structural variables such as socioeconomic status, gender, region and race/ethnicity.
- The figures cited in Table 6.1 are skewed by the decline of the minor party vote. In 1992 and 1996, Ross Perot (who stood as an independent and then as the Reform Party candidate) attracted 19% and 8.5% respectively.
- Some suggest that voting behaviour has become more partisan since the 1990s. In particular, very few Republican voters are now prepared to back the Democrats.
- The reasons for the shift may include:
  - the increase in partisan sentiments generated by the 'conservative revolution' of the 1990s when Congressional Republicans sought to implement the *Contract with America*
  - the bitterness and partisan hostility that grew out of Judge Kenneth Starr's inquiry into President Clinton's conduct and the subsequent impeachment trial
  - the role of Fox News and other conservative outlets in rallying Republican opinion
  - the character of the Bush administration, which has, according to critics, been partisan and confrontational.

Has the USA become more partisan and polarised?

Polarisation

Dan Balz (2005) notes that 'Political polarization intensified during the 2004 elections, continuing a trend that has defined voting behavior for most of the past decade and that has left the two major parties increasingly homogenized and partisan.'

Two nations?

The 2000 and 2004 presidential elections gave rise to descriptions of the USA as 'two nations' or, in other accounts, a 'fifty-fifty' nation. The electoral map seemed to confirm this. There was, it was said, a significant divide between the 'blue' states, which had backed John Kerry (and Al Gore 4 years earlier) and the 'red' states, which supported George W. Bush. 'Blue' states are generally metropolitan in character or are, at least, tied to metropolitan regions. For the most part, they are multi-racial and multi-ethnic. The 'blue' population is younger and more likely to be single. Within 'blue' cities there are liberal enclaves and in some cases visible gay communities (such as Greenwich Village in New York). 'Blue' states lean towards the Democrats.

'Red' states are, again with important exceptions, more rural and are largely white. Although Texas has over 22 million residents, most 'red' states have relatively small populations. They incorporate quintessential small-town America. For this reason, some call them the 'heartland' states. Others are less generous and dismissively refer to them as 'flyover' states.

Those who talk of a divide between the 'red' and 'blue' states cite other parallel developments. These, they suggest, also point to a process of polarisation.

At times, in the past, there was a substantial 'cross-over' vote, particularly among Republicans. It is now relatively small. Voting loyalties appeared, at least at the time of the 2004 presidential election, to have become more entrenched.

In recent years, there has been a decline in 'split-ticket voting'. This is where the voters back a candidate from one party for the House of Representatives and a candidate from the other for the presidency. It reached a peak during the 1970s and early 1980s. It has been closely examined in studies of US politics and its growth was regarded as evidence of partisan dealignment. However, as Table 6.2 shows, split-ticket voting has declined since the 1980s. Again, this seems to confirm the solidification of party loyalties.

Table 6.2   Split-ticket voting

Election year	Number of districts with split-ticket results	% of House seats
1980	143	32.8
1984	190	43.7
1988	148	34.0
1992	100	23.0
1996	110	25.3
2000	86	19.8
2004	59	13.6

Source: adapted from www.rhodescook.com/analysis.html

There is another perspective. The picture of polarisation, and the electoral maps, such as that in Figure 6.1, which have been drawn upon to illustrate it, are misleading. They are derived from the Electoral College Vote. This uses the winner-takes-all system and, in itself, reveals only that there was a simple plurality within a state backing the winning candidate. Beyond that, it says nothing about the size of the minority backing the losing candidate. For example, Florida is designated a 'red' state but it supported Bush by only the narrowest of margins in 2000. In 2004, he gained just 52% of the vote. Those opposing Bush in Florida remain 'unrepresented' on the map and in accounts of 'two nations'.

Figure 6.1 The Electoral College Vote, 2004

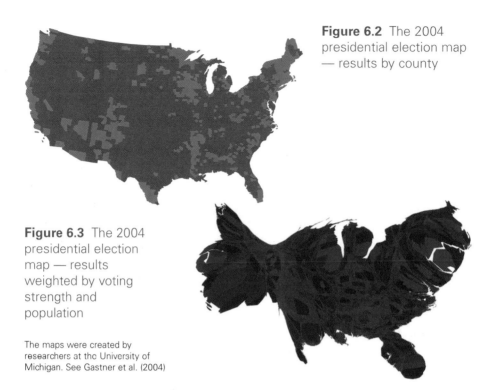

Figure 6.2 The 2004 presidential election map — results by county

Figure 6.3 The 2004 presidential election map — results weighted by voting strength and population

The maps were created by researchers at the University of Michigan. See Gastner et al. (2004)

If counties are used as the basis for an electoral map, rather than states, the picture goes beyond a red–blue divide. Instead, although there are still large swathes of red, the USA begins to look a rather more complex country. There are significant pockets of blue within the red states and large amounts of red within the blue states (see Figure 6.2).

There is still, however, a need to go further so that other variables are considered. The 2004 electoral map needs to be adjusted to allow for (a) the extent to which voters in a particular county backed Bush or Kerry and (b) the relative population sizes of the different states. After all, in terms of population, California (the most populous state) is much more significant than Wyoming (the least populous state).

The map can be adjusted to take account of these factors. The size of the more and the less populous states can be made proportionate. At the same time the colours can be adjusted so that those counties that support Bush or Kerry strongly are shown in dark red or blue while the counties where the vote was less decisive and they had rather smaller leads are depicted in intermediate colours.

Instead of depicting 'two nations', Figure 6.3 suggests that voting loyalties are not as pronounced as it sometimes seems. Although there are clearly defined 'red' and 'blue' counties, many areas are purple. Relatively small swings would lead to a change in the overall result.

'Leaners'

Despite all the talk of polarisation, the evidence to support the claims that have been made is at most patchy. Indeed, depending upon the dates that are used, some of the evidence points to a loosening or weakening of party attachments rather than the intensification of sentiments and loyalties. The Democrats have undoubtedly lost significant numbers of 'strong' and 'weak' identifiers. However, there has been a parallel rise in the proportion of Democratic 'leaners' (those who call themselves 'independent' but 'lean' towards the Democrats). Whereas there were a mere 6% in 1960, 17% defined themselves in this way in 2004. There has also been a rise in the proportion of Republican 'leaners', while the proportion of the population who defined themselves as 'strong' or 'weak' Republican identifiers held broadly steady (despite a falling-away during the 1970s and 1980s). (Note that some research work suggests that many 'leaners' may not really be 'leaners', but instead vote just and perhaps more consistently for their party than identifiers.) At the same time, the proportion of 'independent independents' (those who do not lean towards a particular party and may be regarded as 'genuine' independents) was, despite some fluctuations, the same (10%) in 2004 as it was in 1960. Table 6.3 shows changing patterns of identification with the major parties and can be used to assess the extent to which there has been a weakening of party loyalties.

Table 6.3 Partisan identification, 1960–2004 (%)

	1960	1970	1980	1990	1994	2000	2002	2004
Strong Democrat	20	20	18	20	15	19	17	17
Weak Democrat	25	24	23	19	19	15	17	16
Independent Democrat	6	10	11	12	13	15	15	17
Independent Independent	10	13	13	10	11	12	8	10
Independent Republican	7	8	10	12	12	13	13	12
Weak Republican	14	15	14	15	15	12	16	12
Strong Republican	16	9	9	10	15	12	14	16
Apolitical	2	1	2	2	1	1	1	0

Source: adapted from ANES (2005)

Weak support for the president?

Although President Bush secured re-election in November 2004, his approval ratings (and those of the Congressional Republicans) fell away during 2005 and early 2006. The Iraq war, continuing economic uncertainties, corruption allegation,

Chapter 6

and the apparent failure of the administration to make full and proper preparations for Hurricane Katrina all contributed to this. Bush was unable to secure Congressional backing for his legislative priorities and the Republican Party seemed split down the middle on proposals for immigration reform. Against a background of disillusionment among many grassroots Republican supporters and those who had backed the Bush–Cheney ticket in 2000 and 2004, it was increasingly difficult to portray US politics in terms of two polarised camps. Instead there were growing numbers of waverers and potential defectors to the Democrats.

Is there a 'gender gap'?

Task 6.2

'People are getting much more into two camps' Clark Bensen (www.polidata.org/). Do you agree?

Guidance

- There are always fluctuations in opinion poll findings over a period of time and these fluctuations are not necessarily significant. It is, instead, important to establish whether or not there are trends and understand the character of these trends.
- There may have been a long-term decline in the proportion of Democratic identifiers ('strong' and 'weak' Democrats). This may be tied to:
  - The decline of manufacturing industry and the trades unions, which — to some extent — provided a social basis for the Democrats from the 1930s onwards.
  - The defection of white southerners, who were until the 1960s loyal Democrats. Many turned to the Republicans because they associated the Democrats with desegregation.
  - Others were alienated by the Democrats' identification with liberalism and group rights. They saw the party as soft on issues such as law and order, unpatriotic, and too closely linked with radical movements.
  - A lack of identity. While the Republicans are popularly associated with specific principles such as small government, tax reductions and an assertive defence policy, it is difficult to identify a Democratic philosophy. Nonetheless, while the proportion of 'strong' and 'weak' Democrats has fallen, the proportion of 'independent Democrats' (who are sometimes called Democratic 'leaners') has increased. Put another way, Democratic support seems to have become 'softer'.
- If Republican 'leaners' are included, there has been a small but discernible long-term increase in the proportion of Republican identifiers. In overall terms, there has been a shift from the Democrats to the Republicans but its magnitude should not be overstated.

Task 6.2 (continued)

- If 'leaners' are included, the Democrats still have an advantage.
- There is little evidence to support claims that there has been a process of polarisation among the American voting public. The parties may be more polarised in Congress and in the state legislatures, but this is not reflected in the partisanship statistics.

Task 6.3

Examine the tables below and answer the questions that follow.

Table 6.4 Gender gap (Republican voting), 1976–2004

	2004	2000	1996	1992	1988	1984	1980	1976
% of men voting Republican	55	53	44	38	57	62	55	48
% of women voting Republican	48	43	38	37	50	56	47	48

Source: adapted from CNN (2004) and *The New York Times*, 10 November 1996

Table 6.5 Gender, marriage and parenthood (Democratic vote) (%)

	1992	1996	2000	2004
Married women with children	49	53	47	43
Married men with children	46	45	37	38
Single women without children	61	68	66	63
Single men without children	61	57	51	53

Source: adapted from Galston and Kamarck (2005), p. 31

(a) To what extent is American voting behaviour characterised by a 'gender gap'? Suggest reasons for the gap.

(b) The 'gap' can be measured in other ways. For example, it can be understood as the difference between the proportion of men voting Republican and the proportion of men voting for the Democrats. Suggest other ways of measuring the 'gender gap'. What difference does this make to the character of the 'gap'?

(c) To what extent — and for what reasons — do marriage and parenthood affect voting patterns?

Guidance

- There is a gender gap. Men 'lean' disproportionately to the Republicans. However, it is important to note that, in some presidential elections, a majority of women — as well as men — have voted Republican.

Chapter 6

Task 6.3 (continued)

- Scholars have suggested that women are more likely to value government services because they often carry the burden of family and childcare responsibilities. Others draw upon political psychology to suggest that women are less likely to back the seemingly aggressive and punitive forms of foreign policy associated with the Republican Party.
- The 'gap' could, for example, be measured by looking at the Democratic vote. Alternatively, the allocation of the vote by each gender could be taken in turn. The form of measurement that is used significantly affects its magnitude.
- On some measures, the gender gap narrowed significantly in 2004: 51% of women voted for John Kerry while 48% of women backed George W. Bush.
- There is, however, an important distinction between married and unmarried women and those who are parents and those who are childless.
- The 'marriage' and 'parenthood' gaps are, in part, a function of age. Those who are married and have children tend to be older than those who are single. They also tend to have higher incomes. Furthermore, a higher proportion of whites than blacks are married.
- Married women with children swung to Bush in the 2004 contest. Some observers attributed this to fears of terrorism and concerns for the future of their children. They were dubbed 'security moms'. Other commentators stressed Bush's stand on moral issues. Surveys suggest that moral principles are of particular importance for married women.

In what ways do gender, race and class fuse together?

It would be a mistake to see long-term variables such as gender, race and class as separate and discrete. Instead, they fuse together. Table 6.6 shows that the Democrats have steadily lost support among white men. Because African-American men and women overwhelmingly back the Democrats, figures showing the 'gender gap' mask the differences between white men and white women. About two-thirds of white men back the Republicans.

Table 6.6 Proportion of white men voting Democrat, 1976–2004 (%)

1976	1980	1984	1988	1992	1996	2000	2004
47	32	32	36	37	38	36	37

Source: adapted from CNN (2004) and The New York Times, 10 November 1996

Working-class 'white' vote

The problem for the Democrats is most acute among working-class ('blue-collar') white men. From the 1930s onwards, the Democrats have been seen as the party of those in the lower socioeconomic groupings, particularly organised labour. Many were inspired by President Franklin Roosevelt's New Deal that, they believed, had provided salvation during a period of economic depression and mass unemployment. However, in 2004, many white men in the lowest income groupings voted to re-elect President Bush. Why, then, are the Democrats losing the backing of the white male working class?

Educational issues

Those with few or no educational qualifications (and who failed to graduate from high school) have the most conservative attitudes towards cultural and moral issues.

Table 6.7 Attitudes towards moral and cultural issues, 2002 (%)

	Less than high school	High school	Bachelor	Graduate
Homosexuality: always wrong	76.5	58	41.3	31.6
Abortion: should not be allowed for any reason	70.3	59	53.1	34.2
Against sex education in public schools	26.2	9.2	11	4.3
Pornography should be illegal to all	46.3	37.8	34	33.7

Source: adapted from the National Opinion Research Center (2005)

Conservatism

The shift away from the Democrats began at the end of the 1960s. There was a backlash against the anti-war protests — which were seen as unpatriotic — and new radical movements such as 'black power'. President Richard Nixon's stand against the cultural and political upheavals of the era earned him the backing of many ordinary Americans whom he dubbed the 'silent majority'. In particular, 'white ethnics' — such as Irish-Americans and Italian-Americans living in cities such as Chicago — were concerned by the apparent erosion of traditional values. From their perspective, the Democrats — who had begun to shift towards liberalism — had become the party of 'amnesty, acid and abortion'.

The appeal of Reaganism

Reaganism had a particular appeal to white men, particularly in the lower-

income groups. Some observers suggest that Reagan spoke in a 'masculine' language about confronting the USA's enemies and tackling crime.

Anti-elitism

In *What's the Matter with Kansas*, Thomas Frank takes this perspective a stage further. He suggests that class feelings have been twisted by the Republicans for partisan advantage. The seeming determination of many east coast Democrats to impose liberal policies — such as the abolition of school prayer — upon a majority of Americans in 'heartland' states such as Kansas has created resentment. Anti-elitism — which was once directed against powerful industrial bosses and financiers — is now channelled against leading Democrats, intellectuals, left-leaning identity movements (such as the gay and women's movements), members of Congress and their judicial appointees. For their part, Republicans have portrayed themselves as the guardians of moral traditionalism and the ordinary American. This has enabled them to win votes among manual workers. Kansas, which has a tradition of protests against inequality and the arbitrary power of the employing class, now elects conservative Republicans.

Task 6.4

(a) Why are the Democrats said to have a 'white men problem'?

(b) To what extent are there differences between educational groups in terms of attitudes towards moral issues?

(c) Given these developments, how might the Democrats regain the backing of white working-class men?

Guidance

- The Democrats have steadily lost the backing of white men and attracted only about a third of their votes. The problem is now particularly serious among those in blue-collar occupations.
- Education is the key variable in determining attitudes towards moral issues. Those with higher qualifications tend to be much more liberal.
- There have been calls for the Democrats to adopt a more pro-active strategy towards the 'white working class'. The party's candidates should, it is said, embrace 'economic populism'. It should talk about wages, working conditions and the threats posed by globalisation. Such an approach, however, cuts across the thinking of 'New Democrat' organisations such as the Democratic Leadership Council and figures such as Bill and Hillary Clinton, who call for the adoption of a pro-business course.

What role is played by issues?

Voting behaviour is determined by short-term considerations as well as long-term variables. These include the personalities of the candidates (or, at least, representations of them), the events that have shaped the context within which the election is taking place and, in the case of an incumbent president seeking re-election, 'performance evaluation'.

Personality

In 1988, the Democratic candidate, Michael Dukakis, was portrayed by the Republican campaign as weak. He seemed indecisive on issues such as violent criminality and this contributed, despite an early lead, to his loss of the election. Similarly, in 2004, John Kerry was depicted as a 'flip-flopper'. He had, it was repeatedly said, 'flip-flopped' on key issues such as tax levels and the Iraq war.

Events

The 2004 presidential election was overshadowed by the 9/11 attacks and the Iraq war. These established national security as a defining election issue. Earlier elections were also shaped by particular developments. The 1980 election (between Jimmy Carter and Ronald Reagan) took place against the background of the Iranian hostage crisis, when US Embassy staff in Tehran had been taken hostage by Islamic militants.

'Performance evaluation'

Both President Jimmy Carter (1980) and President Ronald Reagan (1984) were judged, in part, on the basis of the record. For his part, Carter was associated with 'stagflation' and economic 'days of malaise' as well as foreign policy crises. It contributed to his loss of the White House. Despite the recession that marked the early phases of Reagan's first term of office, the economy then began to improve. Reagan's hard-line foreign policy stance also seemed to be yielding dividends. The renewed sense of well-being contributed to Reagan's victory over his Democratic rival, former vice-president Walter Mondale.

Chapter 6

Did issues shape the outcome of the 2004 presidential election?

Yes. In November 2004, George W. Bush secured a second term in the White House and the Republicans maintained their majorities in Congress. Indeed, they made net gains of three in the House of Representatives and won four further Senate seats. The Senate Minority Leader, Tom Daschle, was defeated in South Dakota.

Why did Bush win? Although long-term shifts by groupings that were once loyal to the Democrats played a part, issues were also important. In the immediate aftermath of the election, commentators sought to explain Bush's victory by pointing to the Republicans' emphasis upon moral traditionalism. The exit polls suggested that 22% of voters saw 'moral values' rather than terrorism, the Iraq war or the state of the economy, as the most important campaign issue.

Table 6.8 Presidential election, 2004: the most important issue (%)

Issue	Backing George W. Bush	Backing John Kerry	Backing Ralph Nader
Iraq (15)	26	73	0
Terrorism (19)	86	14	0
Economy/jobs (20)	18	80	0
Moral values (22)	80	18	1
Health care (8)	23	77	*

Note: the columns show the percentages within the groups identifying a particular issue (such as Iraq) as the most important issue, and who they voted for.
Source: adapted from CNN (2004)

What were the key moral issues?

Observers pointed to same-sex marriage. In November 2003, the Massachusetts Supreme Judicial Court had ruled that — under the provisions of the state constitution — there were no rational grounds for denying same-sex couples the benefits and responsibilities of married life. Same-sex marriage became legal in Massachusetts from 17 May 2004. Many traditionalists feared that the federal courts might — if a case were brought — cite the 'right to privacy' or the 'full faith and credit clause' (which requires the individual states to recognise the 'public acts, records, and judicial proceedings' of other states) to establish same-sex marriage across the USA. The 1996 Defense of Marriage Act (DOMA) had assured the states that they had the right to refuse to recognise same-sex marriage ceremonies conducted elsewhere. This measure was strengthened and reinforced by the passage of 'mini-DOMAs' in 39 of the states, which confirmed and reasserted the determination of the states that passed them not to recognise the legitimacy of gay and lesbian marriage.

These anxieties laid the basis for a proposed Federal Marriage Amendment (FMA) to the US Constitution and ballots to amend the state constitutions. While President Bush said little about the issue (although he formally backed the Amendment at the end of February 2004), some Congressional candidates emphasised it, and the Republican Party became closely associated with the campaign to protect traditional marriage.

Same-sex marriage probably did little to win voters across from the Democrats. Most Democrats also opposed same-sex marriage, although nearly all — including John Kerry — argued that an amendment to the Constitution was unnecessary. Furthermore, few issues have sufficient salience to drag voters across the divide between candidates. However, the prospect of same-sex marriage may have acted as a 'mobiliser', drawing white conservative evangelicals — a core Republican constituency — and other churchgoers to the polls. They then voted in overwhelming numbers for Bush. In simple terms, there was 'a super-mobilisation of the Christian right'.

'Moral values' may have shaped the outcome of the election in another way. The 2004 election was — in the words of operatives — both an 'air' and a 'ground' war. Alongside the television and radio advertisements, grassroots activists and volunteers made telephone calls, distributed leaflets and visited homes to register prospective voters. Local church-based groupings and networks — for whom moral and religious values were undoubtedly pivotal — seem to have played a critical role in organising these efforts. The Democrats also increased their turnout levels. Operatives hired by 527s (supposedly independent organisations established to promote an issue or candidates) such as America Coming Together (ACT) campaigned vigorously. Their efforts were, however, more than matched by the Republican volunteers.

Task 6.5

(a) What are 'moral values', and why are there difficulties defining them?

(b) In what ways did moral values contribute to George W. Bush's re-election victory?

Guidance

- In contemporary US politics, 'moral values' usually refer to issues such as abortion and homosexuality. These are seen as important priorities by the Christian right and

Task 6.5 (continued)

much of the Republican Party. However, some observers point out that the term may have other meanings to respondents in opinion polls. They could refer to the ethical principles of politicians or perhaps the USA's relationship with developing countries. Nonetheless, in 2004, 80% of those identifying 'moral values' as their principal concern voted for Bush rather than Kerry. This suggests that they probably saw 'moral values' in the same way as the Christian right.

- Moral values may have pulled white evangelical Christians to the polls, although there is some controversy among political observers about this. They may have encouraged Republican supporters to campaign on behalf of the Bush–Cheney ticket.

Who votes?

The voting-age population (VAP) includes all those who are aged 18 or over and resident in the USA. Most studies of electoral turnout are based upon the VAP.

Task 6.6

Take a look at the table below and answer the questions that follow.

Table 6.9   Voter turnout, 1980–2004 (% of voter-age population)

Year	VAP rate
2004	55.27
2002	36.29
2000	50.01
1998	35.33
1996	48.13
1994	38.50
1992	54.73
1990	36.45
1988	50.34
1986	36.53
1984	53.25
1982	40.73
1980	52.61

Source: adapted from United States Election Project (2004)

Task 6.6 (continued)

(a) Why might some observers argue that the figures shown in the table are misleading?

(b) What trends are evident in the table and what factors might explain them?

Guidance

- Electoral turnout can be measured in different ways. It is most usually represented as the proportion of all those aged 18 or over living in the USA, the 'voting-age population' (VAP). However, this is a misleading figure. The VAP includes non-citizens and those such as convicted felons who have forfeited the right to vote. The VEP (voting-eligible population) offers a rather more useful form of measurement.

- Turnout, particularly if the VAP is used, is low. This has been attributed to the uncompetitive character of many elections, detachment from the civic and political process, obstacles to registration and geographical mobility.

- Turnout is significantly higher in presidential election years. 'Mid-term' elections attract less interest and attention even though the entire House of Representatives, a third of the Senate and many state-level positions are being contested.

- There was a rise in turnout in 2004, although it was barely higher than in 1984 and 1992. This may have been because of polarisation. Many Democrats were fiercely opposed to George W. Bush and his policies, while many Republicans admired and respected him. It could also be attributed to the close character of the contest. In contrast with some earlier elections, the result was far from being a foregone conclusion.

What is 'realignment' and are there 'critical elections'?

Elections are not evenly matched contests. For long periods, according to realignment theorists, one party is predominant. One party wins most of the elections and the other party is subservient. Although the minority party may win elections, it is often compelled to accept the ideology and philosophy of the majority party.

Elections can therefore be divided into two types or categories: realigning and non-realigning elections. Realigning elections (which, although the terminology varies, are sometimes dubbed critical elections) reshape the political landscape: 'a new dominant voter cleavage over interests, ideological tendencies, or issues replaces an old one' (quoted in Mayhew 2002, p. 2). There are many more non-realigning contests. Elections follow cycles. According to Walter Dean Burnham,

they have a 'periodic rhythm'. As Paul Allen Beck puts it: 'Realignments have occurred at roughly three-decade intervals, and each realignment has been followed by a long period of stable normal politics' (quoted in Mayhew 2002, p. 16).

Table 6.10 shows the 'critical elections' that, some observers argue, divide up different periods of party alignment. There is little agreement, however, about developments over recent decades. As noted below, some argue that realignment took place and claim that particular elections were 'critical elections'. Others assert that there have been no fundamental turning points.

Table 6.10 Critical elections

Critical election	President	Dominant party	Regional and social groupings backing dominant party
1800	Thomas Jefferson	Democratic-Republicans	The south and agricultural interests (displacing New England)
1828	Andrew Jackson	Democrats	The south and west — the 'common man'
1860	Abraham Lincoln	Republican	New England, urban immigrants
1896	William McKinley	Republican	Although the Republicans remained in control, the basis of their support shifted to industry, urban dwellers, farmers in the east and Midwest, Catholics, Lutherans, those in the border states
1932	Franklin D. Roosevelt	Democrat	Labour unions, white southerners, African-Americans, intellectuals, Jews, immigrants, farmers (the 'New Deal coalition')
?	?	Republican	White southerners, white evangelical Christians, rural interests, higher income groups, blue-collar male workers

In this context, splits within the major parties and the emergence of minor parties can be an important indicator, particular if the minor parties attract significant numbers of votes. This often indicates that established forms of alignment are breaking up or, at least, are ripe for change.

Between 1896 and 1932, the Republicans were the dominant party. They recruited new and different groupings into the ranks of their electoral coalition including farmers in the east and Midwestern states. The Republican hold was strengthened at the end of the century by prosperity and the Spanish-American war. The party controlled Congress from 1896 to 1930 (except 1910–18). They dominated every region except the south, which was solidly Democratic. The Republicans also occupied the White House, only losing to Woodrow Wilson in 1912 (when the party split) and 1916. However, in the midst of the depression that followed in the wake of the Wall Street crash, the laissez-faire and individualist ideas that many Republicans backed lost their relevance and appeal. In 1932, the Democrat Franklin D. Roosevelt was elected. He won the next three presidential contests and his successor, Harry Truman, pulled off a surprise victory in 1948. The 'New Deal Coalition' that formed the basis of the Democrats' election victories brought together diverse groupings including blue-collar workers (a significant proportion of whom were African-American) and white southerners.

Was there a process of realignment during the second half of the twentieth century?

What happened during the latter half of the twentieth century? There were certainly significant shifts in voting loyalties and the character of the electorate of the kind that are often associated with the realignment process.

The regional bases of support for the major parties have shifted. In the south (which had for a century been so closely bound to the Democrats that it was known as the 'solid south'), the Republicans made major gains. At the same time, the Democrats have made electoral advances in the northern states. As Stonecash et al. (2002) note:

> Each party, to be sure, still wins seats in the regions largely dominated by the other party, but the relative success of each party by region has shifted steadily and dramat- ically over time…The crucial matters are that over the last fifty years the Democratic Party has lost its heavy reliance on the South and became a party based more outside the South. The Republican Party, once heavily reliant on the North, now relies on the South as much as any other region.

What were the reasons for these regional shifts?

Racial desegregation

The Democrats' losses in the southern states can be largely attributed to the process of racial desegregation. For their part, the Democrats were increasingly tied to the desegregationist cause, despite the presence of strident segregationists in their ranks. Following the Kennedy assassination, President Lyndon Johnson called and lobbied for the adoption of the 1964 Civil Rights Act (which ended racial discrimination in the provision of public facilities such as restaurants or trans- portation) and the 1965 Voting Rights Act (which provided federal officials to ensure that African-Americans could vote without fear of intimidation). Although many Congressional Republicans backed desegregation, Senator Barry Goldwater,

the Republicans' 1964 presidential candidate, opposed efforts by Congress and the federal government to end segregation. Although Goldwater did not support segregation and instead spoke of 'states' rights' (the right of the states to make their own decisions) and the 10th Amendment to the Constitution, it seemed to many southern whites and African-Americans that Goldwater and the Republican Party were throwing their weight behind segregation and racial discrimination. These feelings are understandable. The courting of the southern white vote was a conscious political strategy. Goldwater himself spoke of 'hunting where the ducks are.' By this, he meant that the Republicans should seek out the votes of those who were disillusioned with the Democrats because of their increasingly assertive backing for desegregation measures.

At the same time, when African-Americans gained the right to vote in significant numbers through the passage of the Voting Rights Act (which suspended the use of literacy tests in determining the right to vote and brought in federal registrars to register voters in districts where there were low levels of black registration), they became the Democrats' most loyal constituency. Although a significant proportion of the (limited) black electorate had supported Dwight Eisenhower (the successful Republican candidate) in the 1952 and 1956 elections, about 90% of African-Americans voted for the Democrats from 1964 onwards.

Black campaigners demanding the vote in 1963

Other changes in voting loyalties

Alongside these regional shifts, there were other changes in voting loyalties.

Ideology issues

For much of the mid-twentieth century, there were relatively few ideological and policy differences between the parties (at least in Congress). Both included conservatives and liberals in their ranks. Indeed, the most vociferous conservatives, who tended to be long-serving members of Congress representing the southern states, were Democrats. However, generational change as well as Republican gains in the south and west contributed to a process whereby Republican office-holders, candidates and party activists began to take consistently conservative positions, particularly on issues associated with the role of government. They backed laissez-faire notions, endorsed tax cuts and sought to curb government social programmes and regulatory mechanisms. For their part, Democratic elites (as political scientists describe members of Congress and state legislatures and party activists) supported proactive conceptions of government. They voted for increases in welfare provision, job training schemes and other 'tax and spend' programmes. The parties therefore began to appeal to different constituencies. More liberal districts and neighbourhoods (which were mostly in the bigger cities, the west coast and the northeast) backed the Democrats. More traditionalist and conservative areas and regions (and the south has long been the most conservative of the regions) increasingly leaned towards the Republicans.

Economic issues

Economic differences between the parties continued to play an important role during the decades that followed. They were exacerbated by the economic uncertainties that marked the period and growing economic inequality. Arguably, there were growing class-based tensions as the gap between those who are unskilled and those with high levels of education widened. Many in the lower-income groups were resentful about their increasingly limited life-chances and fearful about their employment prospects and living standards. Relative economic security led many in the more successful groups to seek tax reductions, while those at the lower end of the scale hoped to see much greater government interventionism. The Republicans seemed to embrace the free market, at times almost without reservation. 'Reaganism', in particular, represented a resolute commitment to tax cuts and limited government. During the 1990s, Newt Gingrich, Speaker of the House of Representatives, maintained this strategy and the sense of partisanship that was tied to it. While Jesse Jackson's 1984 and 1988 attempts to secure the Democrats' presidential nomination represented the high water mark of the party's radical wing, many other Democrats were committed to some government provision to aid those who were most disadvantaged.

Moral issues

From the late 1970s onwards, moral issues also began to divide the parties. The Republican Party increasingly became associated with traditionalist morality. It was the party that opposed the legal provision of abortion and supported 'pro-family' policies. The Christian right established itself as a significant constituency within the party. Republican presidential contenders actively sought the backing of its 'kingmakers'. At the same time, the Democrats were increasingly tied to identity politics. The party's ranks included those drawn from the women's movement (which vigorously campaigned for abortion rights) and gay activists.

Ethnic group issues

The Democrats had long been the party of the more recent immigrant, whereas the Republicans were traditionally more closely associated with WASPS (White Anglo-Saxon Protestants). Irish-Americans (such as the Kennedy family) were, at least until the mid-twentieth century, among the Democrats' most loyal constituency. The relationship between the Democrats and immigrants, however, assumed greater electoral importance as the number of immigrants grew from the late 1960s onwards. From the 1920s until then, there had been strict immigration quotas. As a consequence of liberalisation, the Latino population has, in particular, grown dramatically. Although many either cannot vote (because they are not US citizens) or do not vote, those who cast a ballot lean disproportionately towards the Democrats. Until the mid-1990s, Asian-Americans, who are also growing as a proportion of the overall population, either did not vote or leaned towards the Republicans. Indeed, they were sometimes hailed as the 'model minority' because of their seeming commitment to work and achievement. However, they too now lean towards the Democrats. This can be attributed to the changing character of the Asian-American population.

There have been sustained efforts by the Republicans at both a national level and in many of the states to court the Latino vote. They have appealed to Latino faith in traditional moral values and the spirit of entrepreneurship. Although George W. Bush and the Texas Republicans made headway, perceptions that the Republicans were hostile to Latino interests (particularly in California) and the apparent opposition of many Republicans to immigration have prevented the party from making greater electoral gains.

Gender issues

There has been an increasingly visible gender gap. From about 1980 onwards, women (particularly single women) leaned disproportionately to the Democrats, while men leaned towards the Republicans. It has been attributed to the Republicans' ever-closer association with 'pro-life' campaigners, the seemingly abrasive policies pursued by President Reagan, the Democrats' emphasis upon education and other forms of government provision and the 'gender-coded' language used by many within the different parties. (Note, however, the narrowing of the 'gender gap' in the 2004 presidential election.)

Where was the realigning or critical election?

Despite these shifts, there are difficulties in attempting to apply the concept of 'realignment' to electoral trends during the latter half of the twentieth century.

Although the Republicans often seemed to be the dominant party, it is difficult to identify a realigning election. Some pointed to Richard M. Nixon's victories in the 1968 and 1972 presidential elections. However, Nixon's successes and the landslide he won in 1972 were not matched by a transfer of power in Congress. Furthermore, in the aftermath of Watergate, the Democrats, under Jimmy Carter, regained the White House in 1976. Other observers saw Ronald Reagan's triumphs in 1980 and 1984 as evidence of realignment. He won the backing of white southerners and many blue-collar workers, which were both traditionally loyal Democratic constituencies. However, although the Senate fell into Republican hands between 1981 and 1987, the Democrats kept their hold over Congress. The picture continued to be mixed in the 1990s. The Republicans won control over both houses of Congress in the November 1994 elections, which (except for a short period between the middle of 2001 and the beginning of 2003, when they lost the Senate following the defection of one of their members) they subsequently maintained. However, Bill Clinton (Democrat) won in both 1992 and 1996. The results of the 2000 and 2004 presidential elections were extremely close. It is tempting to talk of Republican dominance but there is continuing doubt.

Task 6.7

(a) What is meant by the term 'realignment'?

(b) Why are 1896 and 1932 seen as 'critical elections'?

(c) What are 'deviating elections' and what significance do they have?

(d) What is the evidence to suggest that there was 'realignment' during the latter half of the twentieth century?

(e) What is the evidence to suggest that there was no 'realignment' during the latter half of the twentieth century and the concept should not be applied?

Guidance

- 'Realignment' refers to long-term shifts by socioeconomic, ethnic, regional or other groupings away from or towards one of the major parties.
- 1896 and 1932 are seen as 'critical elections' because there was large-scale realignment that led to a switch between dominant parties.
- 'Deviating elections' are those won by the subordinate rather than the dominant party. Often, however, the subordinate will have adopted many of the dominant party's policies and principles.
- Those who suggest that there was 'realignment' during the latter half of the twentieth century point to the Republicans' electoral victories, changing patterns of partisan identification and the acceptance of core Republican ideas, most notably the free market and limited government across much of the political spectrum.

Task 6.7 (continued)

- Those who argue that it is mistaken to talk of 'realignment' during the latter half of the twentieth century emphasise the extent to which the parties are finely balanced (which was evident, for example, in the 2000 and 2004 presidential elections), Bill Clinton's victories, and (during 2006) President Bush's and the Congressional Republicans' fall in the opinion polls. They also stress that only some forms of Republican thinking are accepted by median public opinion. There are still, for example, majorities for (restricted) abortion provision and Social Security provision for the elderly.

What has been said in the commentaries on realignment?

Several US commentators have considered the realignment issue. Most look at the extent to which the Republicans have secured long-term hegemony. Walter Dean Burnham, on the other hand, offers a rather different perspective. Writing at the time of the 2000 primary campaigns, he attaches particular importance to the 'insurgent' candidacy of Senator John McCain, who, he argued, challenged the party establishment's backing for George W. Bush.

Fred Barnes

There's really no reason to wait. Realignment is already here, and well advanced. In 1964, Barry Goldwater cracked the Democratic lock on the South. In 1968 and 1972, Republicans established a permanent advantage in presidential races. In the big bang of realignment, 1994, Republicans took the House and Senate and wiped out Democratic leads in governorships and state legislatures. Now, realignment has reached its entrenchment phase. Republicans are tightening their grip on Washington and erasing their weakness among women and Latinos…Republicans have also surged in party identification. Go back to 1982, the year of the first midterm election of Ronald Reagan's presidency. The Harris Poll found Democrats had a 14-point edge (40 to 26 percent) as the party with which voters identified. By 1992, the Democratic edge was 6 points (36 to 30 percent) and last year, President Bush's midterm election, it was 3 points (34 to 31 percent)…Nothing is guaranteed in politics. The political future is never a straight-line projection of the present. And the ascendant party always hits bumps in the road. Democrats were dominant from 1932 to 1994, but they lost major elections in 1938, 1946, and 1952. Now, Republicans are stronger than at any time in at least a half-century and probably since the 1920s. Realignment has already happened, and there's no reason to pretend otherwise.

The Weekly Standard, 27 October 2003

David R. Mayhew

Electoral politics…is to an important degree just one thing after another…Elections and their underlying causes are not usefully sortable into generation-long spans…It is a Rip Van Winkle view of democracy that voters come awake only once in a generation…It is too slippery, too binary, too apocalyptic, and it has come to be too much of a dead end.

Wikipedia, *Realigning election*, en.wikipedia.org

Walter Dean Burnham

One might be led to think that a political realignment in the country is imminent. In the short term, however, this is unlikely…On the ideological plane, government is perceived in conservative terms, but operationally, there is a liberal mode that favors continuation of domestic programs that only Big Government can provide. And there is no sign that the public at large has any interest in having this contradiction resolved…

History tells us that economic concerns often play a major role in realignments, when they do occur. The long New Deal era arose out of the bankruptcy of an earlier business hegemony over national political and economic life…

The currently blocked system seems to be on, or approaching, its last legs. Its equilibrium becomes more unstable — hence, vulnerable to sudden and explosive overthrow — with every election

…very large parts of the electorate believe their votes to be meaningless. From Ross Perot's huge showing in 1992 to the Republican 'earthquake' of 1994, and on to the persistent increase in the number and proportion of American adults who have opted out of the electoral market altogether, the public has been sending clear signals to that effect…The primary campaigns of 2000 reveal that it is alive and well.

What might it take to produce a progressive realignment? Thoughts turn to the economy. Unless we assume that we have at last repealed the laws of economic gravity, the stock market will at some point fall. In varying ways, depending on their position in the class structure, a lot of people will then be a lot poorer than they are now. Imagine further that when this happens, Republicans are in charge…Democrats might then sweep to power and fashion a new (or recalibrated) political order. This would lead to a positive and proactive role for the federal government in managing the political economy's collective affairs.

…look for a combination of political decisions and economic and/or threatening global stress to trigger a genuine political explosion relatively soon — perhaps toward the end of this new decade, perhaps a bit sooner or later.

The Nation, 17 April 2000

Chapter 6

Task 6.8

In what ways do Barnes, Mayhew and Burnham agree and disagree about the process of realignment in the late twentieth century?

Guidance

Mayhew considers the problems that the concept of realignment brings forth. For his part, Barnes celebrates a Repulican realignment. Walter Dean Burnham believes that the stage is being set for a leftist form of realignment.

Further reading and references

- ANES Guide to Public Opinion and Electoral Behavior (2005) *Party Identification 7-Point Scale 1952–2004*.
- Balz, D. (2005) 'Partisan polarization intensified in 2004 election: only 59 of the nation's 435 Congressional districts split their vote for President and House', *Washington Post*, 29 March.
- CNN (2004) *Election Results – US President/National/Exit Poll*, www.cnn.com
- Galston, W. A. and Kamarck, E. C. (2005) *The Politics of Polarization, (Washington DC, The Third Way Middle Class Project)*, p. 31.
- Gastner, M., Shalizi, C. and Newman, M. (2004) *Maps and Cartograms of the 2004 US Presidential Election Results*, www-personal.umich.edu
- Mattei, F. and Niemi, R. G. (1991) 'Unrealized partisans, realized independents, and the intergenerational transmission of partisan identification', *The Journal of Politics*, vol. 53, no. 1, February, pp. 161–74.
- Mayhew, D. R. (2002) *Electoral Realignments: A Critique of an American Genre*, Yale University Press.
- National Opinion Research Center (2005) *General Social Survey Codebook*.
- Niemi, R. and Jennings, M. K. (1991) 'Issues and inheritance in the formation of party identification', *American Journal of Political Science*, vol. 35, no. 4, November, pp. 970–88.
- Stonecash, J. M., Brewer, M. D., Mariani, M. D. (2002) *Diverging Parties*, Westview Press.
- United States Election Project (2004) *Voter Turnout Statistics*, http://elections.gmu.edu
- Verba, S., Lehman Schlozman, K. and Burns, N. (2003) *Family Ties: Understanding the Intergenerational Transmission of Participation*, www.brown.edu/ Departments/ Political_Science/faculty/Zuckerman/chapter5.pdf